NEW LONGMAN LITERATURE

Kite

Melvin Burgess

PEARSON
Longman
Edinburgh Gate
Harlow, Essex

Pearson Education
Edinburgh Gate
Harlow
Essex
CM20 2JE
England

First published in Great Britain 1997 by Andersen Press Ltd

This educational edition first published by Pearson Education 2005

ISBN 1 405 816465

Printed in China

The Publisher's policy is to use paper manufactured from sustainable
forests

Cover image by Tony Fleetwood

Contents

To the children and staff at Kelbrook School, with special
thanks to Keith Sutton, the bird man

One

There was an ash tree in the churchyard at Hale Magna with a crows' nest in the top. The tree was enormous. It reached up far, far above the church spire and dusted the clouds that drifted overhead. The crows sat on high and cawed down at the churchgoers in their Sunday best. The local landowner, Reg Harris, peered back up and cursed them.

'Bloodthirsty thugs,' he growled to the vicar. But the vicar liked birds nesting in the churchyard and for once Harris was helpless to get his way.

One afternoon, with a slow wind rocking the tree tops, Harris grabbed Taylor Mase as he heaved home a bag of shopping for his mother. He took the boy firmly by the shoulder and pointed with his stick at the nest moving gently in the ash tree.

'Young crows,' he said. He winked. 'You're a monkeyboy. You climb up and bring 'em down for me.'

Taylor stared up at the tree in terror. He knew how to climb trees all right, but this one was as high as heaven!

He hated Harris, with his ugly jokes and bad temper. But Harris was the boss – the Lord High Muck, his dad called him. When it was Harris asking you did as you were told.

Harris handed him a little cotton bag to put the fledglings in and gave him a push-up onto the lowest branches. Taylor sighed with fear and began to climb.

After a long while he looked down for the first time and he almost fell. He was miles above everything! On one side he was on a level with the iron cock on top of the steeple, which now looked huge. On the other the tiny world spread out under the huge sky. You could see forever. Straight down below was Harris's red face peering up from the bright green grass.

The tree swayed slightly. Taylor gulped and buried his head in his arms.

'Don't worry … turf's soft as clay!' called up Harris.

Taylor could hear him snorting with laughter at his own joke. He lifted his head carefully. It felt as though the slightest movement would send him hurtling down. He told himself not to look down again and carried on up.

By the time he got up to the nest, the tree, which had seemed to sway so gently from the ground, was swishing and heaving through the air. The branches creaked and the twigs rattled together and the leaves hissed like the sea. But in a funny way it was peaceful so high up, miles from the world and all its business. Taylor clung to his branch and daydreamed that he lived up here, close to the sky. It would be his own world. It would be glorious.

Far below him Harris shouted but he could hardly hear him. Far, far away the green fields turned into mist. Up in the sky he could see a bird. Taylor knew about birds and he twisted his head curiously to have a better look. But the bird was too high to recognise. Even this tall tree he was riding on must seem as small as moss from such a height.

There was a flap of air and an angry croak close to him. Taylor steadied himself on the branch and turned his head. The crows had come to protect their nest.

They stood on a thick branch a little way off, shuffling closer and closer to him. One of them took off and flapped nearer. It was so close he could see the little feathers at the base of that heavy, black pick-axe of a beak, and an angry black eye. Taylor thought, what if one of them came to peck him?

He shouted at them. They flew up and landed a little further away, but then they began stamping up the branch again, getting closer. Keeping one eye on them, Taylor climbed the last few feet to the nest.

The baby crows had just hatched. They were so ugly it put him off touching them: soft pulpy bodies with thin fluff all over, and big, black, lumpy eyes sticking out. They looked old and dying, not young and full of life. He reached over to take one. He hated hanging on with one hand. The young bird felt hot in his hand. 'What does he want crows for?' muttered Taylor. No one wanted crows. They were just vermin.

He put the birds, four of them, one by one into the little cotton bag Harris had given him. The adults croaked and made little flights at him through the air but they were scared to get too near.

'Sod off!' he yelled and then glanced guiltily down at Harris in case he'd heard. Harris grinned, stuck his heel in the ground and looked the other way. Taylor began to back down the tree.

Getting down was much worse because he had to hold the bag of crows in one hand and look down all the time. The ground at the bottom of the great, long stems seemed to want him, to pull at him. Taylor was sweating with fear. One slip and he could imagine himself banging and bashing and breaking up on the branches as he tumbled down. It would be certain death if he fell.

Halfway down, disaster struck.

He was reaching out with a foot when his hand slipped, his foot went down, he lost his hold. He fell about eighteen inches and landed with a thump on his bum on the branch. Taylor flung his arms around the trunk and stopped himself, but the bag of crows tumbled out of his hand. He hugged the branch and watched it fall; his stomach went with it. It might have been him. It fell a hundred miles going bang, bang, bang against the branches and landed with a soft thump on the turf not far from Harris's feet. The boss gave him an odd look and bent down to pick it up.

Harris would kill him, kill him. Shaking with shock, Taylor climbed carefully back down. Below him, Harris swung the bag from a finger and waited.

'Sorry, sir!' Taylor jumped the last couple of yards and scrambled to his feet. 'Are they okay?'

'Ooooo, I should say not. Bit of a rough ride for the young hooligans.' Harris dangled the bag right in Taylor's face. It was red and wet around the bottom.

'Yum yum,' smiled Harris. He fished in his pocket and came up with a shilling which he flicked at Taylor.

'Good climb. Pity about the crows but it can't be helped. We'd better not tell the vicar, mind, boy. He has a weak spot for them, poor man.'

'I won't say a thing, sir.'

'Good lad!' Harris swung on his heel and marched off, swinging his stick in one hand and the little bag of battered crow chicks in the other. He seemed in good spirits, not cross at all. Taylor couldn't understand what it had all been about. He picked up his shopping bag, which Harris had hooked up on a branch for him, and ran home.

Back home, his mum and dad were drinking tea and listening to the radio. It was 1964 and one of the Beatles first records was playing. Anne Mase was pretending to play a guitar and going, 'She loves you ... oooooo-oooooo!' She had a fringe just like Paul McCartney. His dad had his hands to his face and was screaming like a girl.

'Anne! Anne! I love you!' he wailed.

Taylor stood in the door and groaned.

'What do you think? Will I get to Number One?' asked his mum.

Taylor just rolled his eyes.

'They'll never last. Give me Little Richard any day,' said his dad, and he began to play the table top as if it were a piano.

Taylor's mother was wanting to know what had kept him. She was cross with Harris for making him climb such a high tree, but his dad laughed.

'Those crows've been driving him mad,' he explained. 'The vicar told him they had sanctuary in the churchyard.' He pulled a face just like Harris and mimicked him. 'Sanctuary? Vermin? Don't tell me God likes vermin!'

Taylor laughed; his dad was wonderful ... and so funny!

Tom Mase was Harris's head gamekeeper. It was his job to keep down vermin of all kinds. Crows were known to enjoy a fat, sweet pheasant chick.

'You did him a favour – and me,' said his dad. 'Harris has been on at me to do something about those crows, and the vicar's been telling me to leave them alone. Trapped between one devil and the next, I've been. You did a good job. Dropping them down only saved old Harris from having to bash them himself.' His dad sipped his tea and smiled at Taylor over the saucer. Taylor smiled back

They were on the same side, him and his dad. One day, when he was grown up, Taylor would be a gamekeeper for the Harris family too.

Two

It was Wednesday after school. Taylor and his best friend, Alan James, were stealing through a young pine plantation. Outside the sun shone, but the pines had been planted so close together that the tangle of branches took all the light. In this wood it was always dusk.

In among the trunks the boys crept, like rats in the gloom. They were hunting for owls' eggs.

At home under his bed, Taylor had eight shoe boxes where they kept their collection of eggs. Each egg had a tiny round hole above and below, where they had blown out the inside. The eggs were delicate and beautiful. It was a miracle to Taylor's mother that her son's fat fingers, which broke dishes like hammers, were able to care so wonderfully for something as fragile as a wren's egg.

Nests were so secret. Whenever you felt under the lips of a bank and found the soft round basket with its secret tucked away inside, or discovered a clutch under a hedge, it was like finding a chest of treasure. And then the secret within the secret: the eggs, little miracles like china, full of goodness, waiting to turn into something else. And there were so many to find.

This pale oval was the swift's egg that Mr Kenny the builder took from a nest in a roof he was repairing. This dark jewel was the egg of a nightingale. Apart from its astonishing dark colour, so un-egglike, there weren't so many nightingales about that you could pick them up any time. The birds nested in the darkest, thickest clumps of thorn and the boys had spent ages chopping about inside the thicket before Alan found the hidden nest. It was curled up in a clump of thorns and lined with moss. They came out scratched and bleeding, 'like lumps of butcher's meat', Taylor's mother said. But they had the prize.

They had the eggs of sparrows, robins, swallows, of jays and starlings, thrushes, greenfinches, goldfinches, woodpeckers – all sorts. But the eggs that the two boys treasured above all were those of the birds of prey.

Their greatest treasure on this earth was the egg of a hobby, stolen from an old crows' nest. Taylor's dad had climbed up to poke out the nest, and saved the egg for them. They had kestrels' eggs, too. There was little chance of getting any more, though. Here on Harris's land, birds of prey were hunted to destruction. But there were real prizes still to be had. Taylor and Alan were certain that a pair of long-eared owls were nesting in the plantation, a couple of miles east of Hale Magna.

It was a great place to build a nest, dark and thick. The owl's moaning calls – ooo oooo ooo – had been heard coming from a stand of older, taller pines in the middle of the young pines. They had to be nesting there. The boys were desperate for the eggs. It was just a matter of finding them.

They spent ages creeping about under the low ceiling of the young pines, seeking the older patch of woodland. At last they burst through a rim of brambles. There were windflowers and the light flooded down between the big trees.

Alan let out a long hiss of excitement. Taylor hushed him – he was always too loud! – and they stood still for long minutes peering up among the light brown branches. There was nothing to be seen and so of course Alan wanted to climb the trees for a better look at once.

The trees were clear of branches until about ten feet above the ground, but there was a trick for that. Alan took a short loop of rope from his pocket. He put it on the ground and stepped into it so that it looped over his shoes and under his heels. By putting a foot on each side of the tree he was able to use the rope to grip the trunk.

It only worked for slender trunks, but there was one just the right size growing up amongst the bigger trees. Alan climbed it, looping himself up like a caterpillar, while Taylor stood on the ground and watched anxiously. He knew very well they should stay still and watch, but he had just taught Alan this trick and now there was no stopping him.

Alan had sharp eyes but the owl saw him first. It was standing bolt upright on a branch very close to a trunk, doing its best to look like a clump of wood. When Alan spotted it, it raised its ear tufts and stretched itself into a thin streak. The big, round, orange eyes and sharp face looked fierce. 'You watch it, little boy,' it seemed to say.

Alan clung to the tree and stared into the marvellous eyes. The owl glared back, elongating itself still further until it looked like an exclamation mark. But where was the nest with its treasure of neat round eggs? Taylor and Alan already had the eggs of the barn, tawny and little owls. If they got this one there was only the short-eared to get, and they'd have the set.

He climbed up another few yards. The owl suddenly tucked its head onto its chest and jumped off the branch, gliding off into the younger trees of the plantation.

'There! There! I *saw* it!' hissed Alan down to Taylor, who was desperately trying to see what was going on. He only just got a glimpse of the bird disappearing into the dense, small pines.

Alan came back down the tree like a rocket going backwards.

'The nest's in there, the nest's in there, the nest's in there!' he whooped.

'Shut up! Shut up!' hissed Taylor. Alan was ruining everything! He was certain he'd found the nest site but although they searched the clump of trees where the owl had landed for twenty minutes or more, they found nothing.

Alan had been fooled. The canny owls used the tall pines only as a lookout post and never flew straight from there to the place of secrets. The owl had slipped away between the trees and gone into hiding. It wouldn't come out again now until it was sure the boys had gone.

'That was your fault,' growled Taylor. 'Shouting like that.'

Alan was furious. 'BOO!' he yelled, hoping to make the

birds jump. In the thickets the owls half closed their eyes and didn't move a feather.

'We'll try again tomorrow,' he said.

'No more shouting and tree climbing, then. We should sit and watch.'

'All right, then,' sighed Alan. But it was so hard!

It was getting late – time to get back. Taylor and Alan pushed back into the thickets, going within five feet of the nest, and giving the owls terrors. But the owls sat tight as the boys crashed past. They picked their way over the broken earth, littered with dead branches, until they got to the edge of the plantation and burst out into the dappled light under the tall oaks. They were miles from anywhere and anyone. Now they were free of the little trees they could run.

'Race you!' And they launched themselves along the track, but ...

'YOU!'

'AH!' It was awful! Alan actually fell over with surprise. Taylor looked desperately about to find out what it was.

There was a man. His head was surrounded in a fluff of fine white hair and he was so small, and dressed all in brown, that for a few seconds they thought they'd been caught by some kind of wood gnome. He had wrinkly black eyes, bulging with fury. He pointed his stick at Taylor's nose.

'What do you think you're about? Eh?'

Taylor gulped. 'Looking for eggs, sir.'

'Eggs? EGGS?' snarled the little man. 'What sort of eggs?'

'Owls' eggs, sir. Long-eared owls,' he added, hoping to impress the man with his knowledge.

'Long-eared owls' eggs!' groaned the little man. He lifted his stick and whacked it down hard on top of Taylor's head.

'Ow!' Taylor clutched his sore head and danced.

'You leave the owls alone!'

'Sorry, sir!'

The old man was having trouble stopping himself from hitting Taylor again. He gripped his stick and groaned and turned on Alan. 'You're a pair of thieves!' he hissed.

Alan backed away. 'It's just owls, sir …'

'Just owls! One pair of long-eared owls nesting in five miles and he's after the eggs and it's just owls. You're vermin, the pair of you!'

Taylor scowled at the old man. Vermin was going a bit far. And anyway, who was this angry little man and what right did *he* have to wander about in Harris's woods?

He pointed at Taylor. 'Name?'

'Mase, sir. Taylor Mase.'

'The Mase boy. The naturalist.'

'We're natural bloody pests, sir!' said Alan brightly. It was one of Taylor's dad's jokes. But the old man was too furious to smile.

Taylor was staring in amazement at the little man. He had a soft rosy face, covered in fine wrinkles like a piece of old leather. He had a pair of great, wide ears, curling

12

limply at the top as if they were damp. They popped out of his halo of white hair like pink surprises. He was only a little bit taller than Taylor himself, and suddenly it was so ridiculous standing in the woods being told off by such a weird-looking person that Taylor giggled helplessly.

The man nodded his head to one side.

'Come along,' he ordered.

Alan made to move, but Taylor wasn't impressed.

'I'm the gamekeeper's boy, sir,' he said. 'I'm about a job for my father.' He looked down his nose at the man, as if he were his father telling someone off. The little man stared at him and turned pinker than ever. Taylor decided to push his luck.

'Have you got permission from Mr Harris to walk in the woods, sir?' he asked.

The old man leaned forward. 'I don't need permission, boy. I'm Mr Harris, too. I'm Teddy, the boss's uncle. You'll come along with me.'

The little man marched Taylor and Alan back along a footpath that wound its way past clumps of elder and small bushes. The trees above them sighed in the wind. The undergrowth scratching their legs was wet and shining from a recent shower. The wild garlic was in full white bloom, filling the air with the smell of green onions. They were brushing through a field of it under the trees when one of the owls hooted right behind them.

Taylor forgot everything. He spun round in excitement, only to find himself face to face with the little old man. He pointed his stick sternly down the path. Taylor moaned and did as he was told. This was daft! Why should anyone want to tell him off for stealing owls' eggs?

The owl hooted again, right by his ear. Taylor couldn't resist a peep. But this time the stick came down – CRACK! – right on his head, so hard he screamed, 'Argh!' There was a second crack and a yell as the stick came down on Alan's head, too.

'You keep your faces forward,' the man snapped.

Taylor was getting cross. Maybe he should make a run for it. The old man would never catch him – but Harris's uncle!

No. He was doomed this time.

Then a barn owl screeched behind him. Taylor flinched. Then a tawny owl hooted. Then the long-eared again ... It was like magic! Suddenly the woods were full of owls. The boys could almost hear their wings gliding among the branches. And yet they all seemed to be ganged up behind them. Taylor tried to peer out of the corner of his eye, but he was scared of that stick. It sounded as if the old man had the owls sitting on him, all sorts, hooting and crying.

Taylor began to think: suppose the old man really *was* a gnome? Something extraordinary was going to happen. The owls were teeming in the woods around them. Was it for revenge? They were taking it in turns to creep up close behind and hoot!

And then something HUGE hooted deeply right in his ear. Taylor and Alan yelped in fright and spun round without thinking. The old man was right behind them.

He'd crept up and had his arms lifted in his jacket pockets as if he had wings himself.

'OO-HU!' he hooted. 'OO-HU! OO-HU!' He lifted his coat high and burst out laughing. Their faces were a treat! He danced around, slapping his legs, wheezing and hissing with laughter.

Taylor knew when he'd been had. He smiled shyly and began to laugh, too.

At last the old man recovered and wiped his eyes. 'Oh! Oh, dear me!' he groaned. 'Well?' he demanded. 'What was that one, then? Know it?' He did it again. 'OO-HU!' A deep, strange hoot.

'No,' admitted Taylor.

'I'm not surprised. It's an eagle owl. Not a British bird at all. Now, what about this?'

The old man spent five minutes going through all the hoots, wails, screeches and moans that the owls made, with the boys guessing what they were. Taylor and Alan were delighted and amazed. The calls were all perfect. Taylor's dad was quite good at bird calls, but they'd never heard anything like this.

He finished off the show with the calls of other birds – a series of warbles, whistles, flutes, screams, quacks, grunts and trills. Taylor didn't know half of them. Finally he produced a shrill, mewing call: Hi-hi-heeya!

'No idea,' Taylor said.

'No? No idea? But you may yet, if you're lucky. Now then...'

The small man took off the little grey knapsack he had

on his back and took out a yellow bicycle cape. He unwrapped a book from the cape, spread the cape on the ground under a tree and motioned the boys to sit by him.

Under the trees, side by side, they peered at the pages. It was a bird book. Inside were lively drawings of all the birds of the British Isles, from the tiny goldcrest to the great eagles and swans.

He pointed one out.

'Kestrel,' said Taylor promptly. Taylor and Alan had similar books themselves. They spent hours and hours poring over them, until they knew every bird off by heart. The man pointed at a woodpecker. 'Seen one?'

'Yup! Green woodpecker.'

'What about this?'

The old man went through half a dozen birds, before he settled on the hawks and falcons. He went through them one after the other and, as he did, he told their story. How gamekeepers and egg collectors had hunted the eagles out of their eyries, the kites from their nests. How the government had paid a bounty to kill peregrines during the war, to stop them hunting carrier pigeons. He told how the pesticides sprayed on the land passed from the crops into the small birds and mice they preyed on, and then into the bodies of the birds of prey. With every mouse or little bird they ate, they took a little more poison, and at last they died. All of them now were rare. Even the once common sparrowhawk was now almost gone.

'These wonderful birds will soon all be gone if we just let things go on as they are. Something has to be done,' lectured the old man. And now the owls' numbers were falling, too. Perhaps it wasn't so clever to steal the eggs of the last remaining few.

Taylor was impressed. He'd never seen anyone who knew so much about birds, not even his dad.

'But it's no use, sir,' he said. 'This is shooting land. We breed pheasants. We can't be having birds of prey round here.'

'Mr Harris will never let them live here,' Alan agreed.

'He has no choice,' snorted the old man. 'It's the law now, boy. Even Harris has to keep the law.' He winked. 'And I intend to see that he does.'

The old man turned the pages of the book and showed them another bird, a great red bird, with a white head and shoulders.

'What about this?' he asked.

They knew it all right. This was the most fabulous, the most famous – and the most desperate – of all the British birds. Every bird lover knew of it and its story. A couple of hundred years ago they'd been common, but now they were so rare they'd almost become a thing of myth, like the unicorn. There was just a tiny handful left in a secret valley in Wales. No one knew where; it was the most closely kept secret you could imagine. The nests were guarded like treasure. And it was treasure that their nests contained. The eggs were worth a fortune.

'Red kite,' said Alan quickly, proud to get it in first. But Taylor was still staring at the page. Alongside the picture of the kite on a branch was a smaller picture of the bird in flight, seen from below. It was unmistakable; the tail was deeply forked. And Taylor had a sudden flash of memory – back a few weeks before when he was robbing the crows' nest for Harris. At the top of the tree when he had looked up, he had seen a strange bird on high. In his memory, clear as day, Taylor saw the bird again. Clear as day.

It had a forked tail.

Taylor felt a sudden, electric thrill go through him. He knew why this old man was here in these woods; he knew why he had made so much fuss about him stealing the eggs.

'Ever seen one of them?' asked the old man.

'Never,' said Taylor with his heart beating like a drum. 'You never see them.'

'Rarest bird in the country! Only twenty-four left.' The old man's eyes were damp with excitement. 'Imagine! One bad winter, a couple of egg collectors, and they could be gone forever.' He pointed a lean finger at the boys. 'What if one of those was nesting near here? What then? Would you rob their nests for the eggs?'

'Oh, never! We never, never would, would we, Taylor!' insisted Alan.

'Never!' exclaimed Taylor indignantly.

He was certain there must be kites nesting nearby.

The old man sent them off with an order to leave the nests alone and an offer to take them out birdwatching some time. Both of the boys were impressed with Teddy Harris. Apart from the fact that he seemed far too nice to be related to Harris, he had such an enthusiasm for birds, just like they did. But although Alan would have jumped through hoops for him already, Taylor could only think about the kites.

As soon as they were on their own he told his theory to Alan. Alan was a couple of years younger than Taylor and he could be made to believe almost anything. But this time he was doubtful. Kites in Hale? Father Christmas, ghosts behind the wardrobe, treasure buried in the garden, maybe. But kites in the woods? Alan was too old to believe that sort of nonsense.

'It's true,' insisted Taylor. 'What's that old bloke doing here, then? Why'd he show us the kite in the book, then? Anyhow, I *saw* it. When I was up that tree for Harris, I *saw* it.'

'They only live in Wales,' said Alan stubbornly.

'I *saw* it. It was here.'

'But, Taylor…'

'It had a forked tail.'

'Wow…'

'Definitely.'

'Wow. *Wow!* Do you really think so, Taylor?'

'This must be their chance to spread out of Wales.'

'Taylor!'

'Right here, in Hale.'

'*Wow!*' Alan goggled. He was always getting wildly carried away but Taylor was the level-headed one. Taylor never told lies, never believed anything unless he saw it himself. If Taylor said it, it *must* be true.

'*Wow,*' said Alan. 'Wow! WOW!'

The two friends spent the next week going through the woods tree by tree. They spent hours sweeping the skyline, searching for the sleek brown-red bird with its buoyant flight and that distinctive forked tail. They crept down the lanes, they climbed trees, they peeked over hedges. They even put down rabbits as bait. Just to catch a glimpse! Just to find a feather!

They saw nothing; they found nothing. Such a big bird, that flew so high above the trees – but there was not a trace. The kites, if they had ever been here, must certainly have moved on.

Taylor was furious with himself for getting carried away like a little kid. Kites in Hale! He must have been off his twig.

Three

Taylor's father, Tom, began his rounds at half past five every morning. The world at that hour was so still it looked fresh-made, the wet dew still on the grass and the sun slowly rising to warm the world and bring it to life.

'God visits just before dawn. Can you smell Him?'

'Can I see Him? Will He call at our house?' Taylor used to ask when he was just a toddler.

Tom would wink at his wife. 'No, but you might find His footprints on the front lawn one day,' he lied. Taylor ran round to look for signs of God in the dew, while Tom pushed open the white painted gate that led into the woods. With his gun over his arm and his dog Sally at his heel, he walked away into the trees slung with mist and ringing with birds.

He had to get his little son away before he left. Taylor would scream for half an hour, he wanted so much to be with his dad.

These days, on mornings when there was no school, Taylor often went with him.

It was spring. Apple blossom in the garden, bluebells in the woods and little brown and grey birds bursting their hearts in song in the thickets. House martins nesting under the eaves.

Spring: the season of eggs.

This time of year found the keepers bending along the hedgerows, searching for clutches of pheasant eggs. A nest could contain fifteen or more greenish-brown eggs, hidden among last year's brown grass stalks.

In these woods, the pheasants ruled. 'Their Darling Little Lordships,' Tom said. His whole life was spent caring for them.

'Chickens with wings,' replied his wife, which made Tom bristle. He was as proud as an emperor come the great days in autumn when the woods were full of bright, healthy birds.

Taylor was brilliant at finding the eggs. He had the eyes for it, his dad said. The egg-filled hollows among the grass seemed to call to him. Whenever he and Tom went out together, Taylor always ended up with as many eggs in his basket, sometimes more.

The eggs were carried back to coops in clearings in the woods, where they would be sat by captive pheasants. They were far too important to be left out in the open. The chicks would be six weeks old and able to care for themselves before they could be put back into the woods. Even then they would be fed regularly to make sure they didn't stray and to stop them getting too wild.

Finding the eggs and caring for the chicks was only half the problem. There were others living in the woods who were just as keen to be there first. The farmer kept his hens in a shed to keep them safe. But who was going to protect the young pheasants when they crept into the woods on their own, or roosted on the low branches of trees at midnight? In the woods, on the fields, in the sky, under the ground, there lived the little hunters. When the woods were full of sweet young birds they attracted the vermin from miles around looking for an easy meal.

Vermin. Rats, weasels and stoats, jays, crows, magpies and hawks: it was everywhere.

After they had collected the eggs and put them safely away in the coops, Taylor and Tom went to check the traps. In between caring for so many little lives, they had a great deal of killing to do.

There were thirty traps to check, morning and evening. There were wire snares for the rabbits, which Tom hid in the runways in the undergrowth and at the entrance to their burrows. Tom hung the little bodies over his shoulder. On a good day he'd go home dressed in a cape of soft rabbits. The rabbits were put on the train for London and market, where they ended up as someone's dinner.

The money for them went to Harris, of course. The land and all it produced – crops, birds, beasts, even the weeds and the insects, even the soil and the stones, even the dust that blew across it and the rain that fell on it – all belonged to him.

Stoats and weasels were caught in spring traps, like mousetraps but bigger. They were baited with the guts of a bird or a young rabbit. The vermin had to stand on a little plate to reach up for the bait – *Snap!* The trap was sprung; the back was broken.

Sometimes the weasels and stoats were caught alive in spring-door traps. Then you had to kill them with a rap on the head with a stick. Tom and Taylor bashed them once more against the trunk of a tree before they tucked them in their bags, just to be sure. They were tough little customers, the weasel tribe. The last thing you wanted was to pop your hand into the bag to take them out and get bitten.

One of the ferrets Tom kept at home to go after rabbits had once jumped out of its cage and taken Taylor's mum by the nose. His dad had to strike a match and set fire to its tail before it let go. His mum had a pink scar on her nose to this day.

It was a good thing the weasels were so small. Taylor liked to imagine what it would be like if they were as big as lions.

'Knock one down, another pops up,' said Tom. He looked slyly at Taylor and put on Harris's voice. 'What's the point of all this *filthy vermin*!' he hissed. Taylor laughed. But it was true. Tom and the other keeper, old John, did their rounds day after day but there was never an end to the stoats and weasels, rats, crows and other pests. Nature was endless; you left the tap full on all day and, when you came back, there they were, still pouring out of it.

In the damp woods below the corner of Short Acre meadow stood the wreck of a long wooden shed. It used to be used as a store in the days before the war, when there had been six keepers looking after the estate. Nowadays, it was used as a gibbet.

The vermin hung, row after row after row of them along the damp sides of the old shed. Each species was nailed up together. Yards and yards of magpies hung by their feet, the recent ones in glossy blue-black and white, the older ones a clammy mess of feathers, mouldering flesh and bones. After them, a long, dark queue of crows, waiting to turn green and rain their little bones onto the grass. Then, the splendid jays. A couple of sparrowhawks hung to the earth, their yellow beaks agape and their broad wings musty and damp. Ten years ago there would have been a dozen or more, but now they were only rarely seen.

Stoats and weasels were nailed up by their noses, as were the rats, their wonderful long tails hanging down. The newer ones were fresh and furry, the older ones wrapped in a shroud of green slime. The fox was present by his beautiful white-tipped tail. The whole body stank too much to hang up.

Everything that lived in the woods was here, except the rabbits, who had another fate, and, of course, the pheasants. It was in their name that this church of death stood. But even they had their turn to come.

Around the clearing grew wild rhododendron trees, and under their branches the earth was disturbed. There were graves here, too. Not all vermin could be hung up.

It happened often enough.

'Have you seen my tabby, Mr Mase?'

'No, but I'll keep an eye open, Mrs Wright.'

But Tabitha lay buried under a hedge. A cat could wreak havoc among the young birds. There were traps for cats –

and dogs. If a cat began to nose in the wrong place, the traps would be set, or the guns would speak and puss would disappear.

Taylor was well used to the gibbet, although he would never have dared come to it after dark. For the keeper it was simply an advertisement for his work. Harris was known to stop his car by the cornfield and walk across two or three times a week to see the gibbet, and make sure his keepers were busy.

Taylor took a hammer from a loop of wire on the wall, pulled a weasel out of his pouch and banged a nail through its nose. He was about to go on to the next one when Tom interrupted him.

'Go and have a look round the end of the shed first,' he told him.

'What is it?'

'Maybe you can tell me.'

Excited, Taylor dropped his hammer and ran round to have a look. From time to time exotic creatures appeared on the gibbet, usually shot by the other keeper, old John. John seemed to think that anything that moved only did it to get at the pheasants. Taylor had seen such harmless things as woodpeckers and hedgehogs, which John claimed sucked the eggs, and even snakes and bats hanging there.

He skidded on the grass at the corner of the shed and almost fell over with surprise. He couldn't have been more shocked if he'd found a man nailed to the gibbet.

Hanging by its feet among the sparrowhawks and owls

was an enormous bird. Its huge wings spread open as if it had been crucified upside down. Blood dripped from the open beak and left a spatter on the grass below.

'Ain't she a beauty?' Tom followed him around to admire the kill. 'I got her over Downlings. Bang! Down she came!'

'*You* did it?' Taylor glanced over his shoulder to check they were alone. Could it really be that his wonderful father had done this dreadful thing?

'Bang!' said his father again. 'Half a mile off, she were. Broke a wing and she was running along the hedge like a chicken. Took her with the second barrel. Well, Taylor, you're the bird man. Any idea what it is?'

The bird was so huge it made the sparrowhawks and kestrels and owls look like robins. Its plumage was the colour of burnt earth. Its head and shoulders were mantled with white. You could see the tongue hanging stiffly inside the yellow and black beak. A fly sucked at its clammy eye. The long elegant forked tail pointed slightly to one side.

It was a red kite.

Taylor could hardly speak. Only twenty-four left, Teddy had said! And now …

'But it's a kite!' he exclaimed

His dad frowned 'Rare, aren't they? Good job I bet one of them could get a fair few pheasants down it.'

Taylor licked his lips. 'We'd better hide it…' he began.

'No, Harris'll want to see it!' his dad exclaimed.

'No! It's illegal! His uncle's here, he's bird mad, he…'

His dad walked across and pulled at one of the long

27

wing feathers. The wing opened like a machine. 'Big as a buzzard! What a shot!'

'It's a kite! It's important. You can't shoot them. They're so rare, you see. They're so few left. Harris's uncle told me. He's come here just because of this bird. And now...'

Taylor babbled on, trying to show his dad that this bird, of all the birds in the sky, was different. His dad would get the sack; he might even go to prison. Harris wouldn't think twice about getting rid of his dad if it suited him.

But Tom just shrugged. 'It's a hawk, a killer,' he pointed out. 'Does a farmer keep a fox with his chickens? Does a man who keeps mice let the cat in?'

Taylor scowled. Did his dad really think that this bird was just vermin, like the rats that crawled about under the gibbet? The kite was like a kind of angel in his mind. So rare ... so big ... so beautiful!

Then behind them they heard a loud, out-of-tune whistle. Harris was making one of his visits to check up on the gibbet. Taylor froze. Just what he was dreading most of all! Harris's temper was famous. When he saw that his dad had been breaking the law like this all hell would break loose.

The bushes parted and they turned to see the hairy red face pushing through. Harris stretched his lips into a wide smile and nodded at Tom.

'Good morning, Mr Harris,' said Tom. He spread out an arm and proudly showed him the huge red bird hanging from the wooden wall. Taylor winced.

Harris stared at the kite. He raised his eyebrows mildly.

'Any idea what you've got hanging up there, Mase?' he asked.

'Taylor says it's a kite, Mr Harris. I've not seen one before, myself.'

Harris rolled his eyes and shook his head tiredly, as if he was dealing with a stupid boy. 'That thing goes under the hedge with the cats and dogs, Mase,' he barked. 'Look at it, hanging there for the world to look it. You ought to have more sense, man.'

Tom's face went blank. 'I'll get it buried, then, sir,' he said. He took his knife out and sawed through the string around the feet. Harris leaned on his stick and watched.

'I've got my mad Uncle Ted on my heels,' he explained. He winked at Taylor. 'He's like you, bit of a bird brain. Nosy little squirt. Spends his time galloping about saving birds. Tells me I'm obliged to put up with a colony of these things nesting on my land. Look at it! Big as an eagle! I said, what about my birds? Can't have those things getting fat on my birds. No, no, he wouldn't have it. Red kites this, red kites that. You'd think the thing was worth money, the way they go on.'

'Sorry to hear it, Mr Harris,' said Tom.

'Filthy things have a nest up by Gordon's Tower. See to it, will you?'

'Will do, sir.'

'And do it quietly, Mase.'

Taylor suddenly found his breath. 'Sir...'

Harris turned to look at him. Taylor felt like vermin himself. He gulped.

29

'Sir ... there're only a few left. Twenty-four. In the whole country. I mean ...' He turned to look at the dead bird. 'I mean, twenty-three now, sir.'

Harris pursed his lips and squinted down his nose at Taylor. 'I see you've met my uncle,' he observed.

'Sir...'

'Well, we're all going to have to be extra careful. He'd shop you for the sake of a sparrow. If he'd seen that bird, Mase, I'd have had to let you go. Mum's the word.'

'Sir...'

Harris turned and eyed Taylor up and down. 'Tell you what. Tell you what ...' He got down on his haunches and smiled like a friend. 'We don't want your dad getting into trouble, do we? So why don't you get up to that kite's nest and poke it out for me? And there's ten bob in it for you. Wages for workers.'

But Tom interrupted. 'I'll see to that job, Mr Harris,' he said.

'Nonsense, it's better if the boy does it. No one's going to prosecute him, are they?'

'If it's against the law, sir, I'd rather keep Taylor out of it.'

'Oh, would you?'

Tom carried on digging but glanced at his boss out of the corner of his eye. 'I don't mind him helping out, Mr Harris, I'm glad of the help. But I don't want him mixed up in anything illegal. I'll take the risks if there are any going.'

Harris nodded as if he understood. 'Still, I think it would be better if the boy did it, Mase. He who pays the piper. Mmm?'

Tom stood up and looked straight back. 'You're the boss, sir, and I do my job. But as far as Taylor's concerned, he's my boy and I'm my own man, Mr Harris.'

There was silence. Harris looked as mild as milk. He said quietly, 'But I don't pay you to be your own man, not in my time, Mase. I pay you to be mine.'

Tom shrugged and got back down to his digging. Harris stood and watched him work on for a few moments before he turned and walked away. In a moment the whistling started up again. No one was fooled. Harris hated to lose his temper, but inside he was livid.

'Go and get on with your weasels,' snapped Tom.

Taylor ran round the back to nail up the vermin, while his father finished off burying the kite. Afterwards, he ordered his son to keep well away from the nest.

'I'll see to that, never mind what Harris says.'

Taylor nodded. His dad was white with anger. No more was said about it.

Four

Gordon's Tower was a round stone tower built a hundred and fifty years before. It was a folly; it had no use but to be looked at, and looked from. If you climbed to the battlements on the top you could see for miles. The top of the hill where the tower stood was overgrown with brambles and young trees, but on the lower slopes were full-grown trees. At the bottom of the hill, in a dip in the land, where the crowns of the trees were hidden by the surrounding wood, the kites had built their nest in a slender oak tree. It was the first nest built by kites outside Wales in over thirty years.

Taylor stood at the foot of the slender grey trunk of the oak tree. Even though he was alone he felt a thousand eyes on him: Teddy Harris, Alan, and every bird in the woods. Everything alive seemed to be judging him.

He reached out and touched the rough bark.

He thought: this tree of all trees. This place, these hands, this boy. Above him sat a kite on her eggs. Even in Wales there were only a handful of such nests. The tree was holy.

But Taylor had not come in praise. He felt sick with greed. He stared up into the trembling green canopy. He tried to soak everything in; he wanted to remember this moment forever. But he was too scared to concentrate. The eyes in his imagination disturbed him.

For a happy moment he thought he was going to be too

scared to do it, but then he thought: they're going to kill it anyway.

He was only following orders. He put a foot on a cleft in the trunk and began to climb.

Harris had found Taylor the day before as he walked home from school. He clicked his tongue sympathetically and put an arm on his shoulder as they walked together down the road. 'Pesky relatives!' he said. 'Pesky, pesky relatives! My uncle, your dad. What a pair!' He grinned and chuckled without amusement. 'Tell you what, though ...' He bent close to Taylor's ear. 'I'm a little worried about your father,' he said in a little worried voice. 'I'd hate my uncle to catch him at that nest, you see. He'd be out of a job; you'd be out of a house. It is my house you live in, after all.' He smiled and winked. 'It's better for you to do it, you know. Of course your dad just has your best interests at heart. But I'm thinking of him. Here ...' He took a ten shilling note out of his pocket and stuffed it into Taylor's pocket. 'Tomorrow afternoon. It's all clear. Uncle's away, your dad'll be busy. I'll see to that.'

Harris stood up, winked, and was gone before Taylor could say a word.

Taylor knew it wasn't right and he hated Harris all the more for going behind his father's back. But he knew at once he was going to do it anyway. And not for Harris, either, although the ten bob would be handy. Taylor was doing it for himself.

He wanted those eggs more than anything else on earth.

As he climbed, Taylor had a picture in his mind of the moment his head would appear over the edge of the nest. It would be a page from a history book. There would be the great bird, caught in her secrecy. He would stare at her and she would start out of her nest like an eagle.

But of course the kite heard him coming. She left the nest almost as soon as he lifted off the ground and all he caught was the briefest of glimpses. A great shape disappeared silently behind the branches as he turned his head. Taylor groaned in disappointment. He had missed the only chance he would ever have to see a live kite close up.

He continued to climb, pushing through the bright green leaves, until at last his dusty, pale face came up by the edge of the untidy nest and he looked down into the holy place.

Three perfect eggs.

Taylor reached out a trembling hand to touch them. They were still warm with the heat of the kite's body. They were alive.

For a few seconds, Taylor soaked up the warmth and stared at the beautiful chocolatey markings on the shell. Then he picked the eggs up and carefully nestled them one after the other inside his shirt. He put them next to his skin as if he had come to care for them. Then he began to climb down.

Taylor had stolen up to the nest, but now that it was done he wanted only to get away. He scrambled down the tree and jumped the last few feet to the ground. On his belly the eggs cracked together. He closed his hands loosely about them and began to run, jumping over logs and fallen branches, skidding on the damp forest earth. He tore along in a rage. His hands cradled the eggs, but every time he heard them crack together he was glad. He hated them for what they had made him do, and for what he was going to do. He'd have thrown them away if he could, but he loved them too, and he was unable to stop himself going through with it.

As the boy fled, half a mile above him the kite flew west. The last kites were shy creatures who had learned to abandon their nests at the slightest danger. She flew fast and never looked back. She would never return.

Taylor's mother was hanging out the washing when he came in, and he was able to sneak past the bright white sheets without her seeing him. Upstairs he half drew the curtains, not that anyone could see in, before he carefully took the treasure from inside his shirt. He hardly dared look. He had treated them like rubbish, running like that!

Somehow, two of the eggs had survived his run without any harm at all. The third had two craters in it, one above and one to the side. Taylor traced the marks with his finger. There was no wet. Although the shell had been crushed the membrane beneath it was unbroken.

Taylor tossed the egg to one side in disgust. It was useless for his purposes; he was only interested in the shell.

Inside each egg lay a little hidden figure. Though they were as still as stones, the eggs were alive. Three tiny hearts beat as fast as a trembling leaf. With a stethoscope,

Taylor would have been able to hear them. If he had held them to a bright light he would have been able to see their shadows, and watch how they trembled and moved inside. They had been brought to life by the warmth of their mother's breast, and kept alive this last half hour by the warmth of Taylor's skin. Now, as they lay on the quilt, a little breeze stirred the curtains and blew across them. The eggs began to cool. As they cooled, they began to die.

Taylor was so anxious it felt as if someone was mincing his insides. He walked round the room bent double, holding his stomach. Then he knelt by the bed in front of the eggs and screwed his fists into his eyes. He stayed there for nearly a minute trying to think of nothing, but he kept seeing Teddy Harris standing in the woods, with his passionate, damp eyes.

'Rarest bird in the country! Only twenty-four left. One bad winter, a couple of egg collectors … and they could be gone forever.'

Taylor was nearly weeping. But then he hissed to himself, 'Don't be so *stupid*. Someone would have killed the kite and taken the eggs anyway. I've probably done it a favour. It'll fly away back to Wales now.'

He went to the cupboard to get out his equipment.

Taylor laid his tools on the table and turned on the little lamp. He took the first egg from the bed and sat down to work.

The main tool was a sharp hatpin his mum had given

him. He carefully chipped away at the top of the egg with the pin until he had made a tiny hole. Then, ever so gently, he pushed the hatpin inside.

Unseen behind the hard shell, the tiny kite half opened its beak, but it lived in a liquid world and it died without a sound.

Frowning, Taylor began to stir the pin about. It was lumpy. That meant the chick had begun to grow. Blowing it would be difficult.

He spent nearly a minute stirring and poking with the pin, trying to break up the half-developed chick. He turned the egg upside down and made a tiny hole at the other end. In here, too, he stirred. Then he held the egg over a white china mug, pressed the hole to his lips, and began to blow.

A thick trickle of bloody muck oozed out of the hole. A vein appeared, doubled up. It got stuck. Taylor blew harder. The vein bulged, then ran out in a lump. He took another breath and blew again.

Something was stuck tight.

Taylor's hands had started shaking again. After all this, it had to work, it had to! He tried stirring with the pin again before another blow, but nothing moved. He tried again with the pin. He blew harder; a little more oozed out. He blew harder … harder …

Taylor was so tense that his fingers tightened without him noticing. The egg crumpled in his hand without warning and a mangled clot fell into the cracked white mug.

Taylor dropped the crushed shell and danced like an imp silently around the table. Why had he done this?

He was ruining everything!

There were two remaining eggs on the bed, their hearts still beating. One egg was ruined; that meant there was only one chance left to add a kite's egg to his collection.

But there was another way to go about it.

Taylor gave way to the thought that was at the back of his head the whole time. He could give the egg to Teddy Harris! He would hatch it, rear the chick, let it go. Then everything would be okay. There would be another kite in the world to make up for the one his dad had shot. Taylor would have saved the eggs, not ruined them. He wouldn't even have to say he had tried to blow them. It was the right thing to do!

He went to touch the eggs. They were noticeably cooler. He took the second egg over to the table and picked up the hatpin.

This time he spent several minutes stirring the insides about, trying to make it all as fine as he could. But although the pin was sharp at the end, the sides were round and couldn't really cut anything up. He tried stirring with the point at different depths into the egg and scraping gently against the inside of the shell. At last he was ready to blow it.

He lifted the egg to his lips and blew, and almost at once his fingers squeezed together and the egg burst in his hand.

Taylor held his head and wept.

After a long time he opened his eyes to stare at the two minced, half-grown forms lying in the bottom of the mug. They were far more than a network of veins; they had begun to form organs. He hadn't stood a chance.

He turned and glared at the third egg lying on the bed. He was furious with it. He rushed over and bounced violently on the bed so that the egg rolled right up close to his knees. What use was it to him if he couldn't blow it? He jumped again. The egg might as well be smashed! He bounced up and down, harder and harder. But at the last moment he caught himself. He felt the egg press lightly against his skin. If he lifted his hands, it would be all over.

Tenderly, Taylor lowered himself to one side of the egg and cupped it in his hand. The egg was quite cool now. It had been lying on the bed for half an hour. Taylor dearly wanted to destroy it, out of anger and also because it was proof of his crime. But in the end, he loved it too much.

Putting the egg in his pocket he ran downstairs and out into the garden. A chicken coop lay in the shade of a holly hedge. Inside was a broody hen sitting on her eggs, bringing on next year's layers. Taylor opened the coop. The hen looked nervously at him. She rolled her eyes and clucked softly, but she was far too much in love with her own eggs to move.

Gently, Taylor eased the kite egg underneath her. The hen shifted and then settled back down on it. As he closed the door she sank low onto the eggs and fluffed up her feathers.

Taylor stood outside and sniggered to himself. What a treat! He'd love to be around to see that hen if the egg hatched. A whacking great kite chick – like a sheep bringing up a wolf!

But of course the egg would never hatch. It was cracked, the chick inside was certainly dead. Even if it was alive the hen would tread on the damaged egg and break it. But he couldn't throw it away.

Taylor heard his mum in the kitchen. He ducked down behind the raspberry canes and sneaked away.

He ran out of the gate and down to the village to call for Alan. He wanted to tell him about his adventure, but he knew at once he never could. He'd just say he'd been looking for the kites but had seen nothing. No one must ever know what had happened that afternoon.

Five

The following Monday morning, Harris was waiting for Taylor in the drive as he made his way to school. He laid his stick firmly on his shoulder to hold him in place.

'Ho, ho, ho. Partners in crime,' he breathed. 'Well done! We'll make a gamekeeper of you yet.'

'Sir,' said Taylor.

'Uncle Teddy is furious,' said Harris with a broad smile. 'Always nice to get one over, isn't it? Of course he tried to blame me ... *and* he tried to blame your dad. But I stuck up for him. I said, "Mase has his instructions and he'll carry them out, he's a good man!" I said. Ho, ho, little does he know.'

'I'd better get to school, sir,' began Taylor.

But Harris leaned down on his shoulder. 'Now then,' he said. 'But what about the eggs? Did you keep 'em?'

'No, no I didn't. I smashed them up, sir.'

Harris scowled. 'Didn't put them in your collection, then?' he asked, grinning widely. 'Kites' eggs. Rare birds. Star prize! Bit of a temptation.'

'No, sir - that'd be too risky, wouldn't it?' Taylor replied, looking him straight in the face.

'Hmm. My land - my eggs. Worth a bit of money, they are. Quite sure, boy?'

'Quite sure, sir.'

Harris grunted and scowled. 'Well, well. You're not entirely to be trusted of course, since you've already shown yourself to be a bit of a turncoat, hm? Still, no point complaining about my own handiwork!' He grinned and ground his heel into the gravel. 'Well. Anyway. Remember – partners in crime. I wouldn't want this getting out. My Uncle Teddy is a complete crackpot, he'd have the law on us in a second. I'm counting on you, and so's your dad. His job depends on it. And your house, of course. Shake on it!'

He held out his big hand and Taylor had to shake as if they'd made some sort of deal. Then Harris lifted his stick with a flourish, and Taylor slunk off to school.

All the way he was thinking – that egg in the hen coop! How had he been so stupid! His mother could find it. And what on earth would happen then?

All day at school Taylor worried about the kite's egg. When he got home his father was working in the garden and he couldn't get near the coop, but at least it hadn't been discovered – yet. With a bit of luck the hen would've eaten it. After tea he went up into his room, from where he could spy on the garden and see when the way was clear. But before he could get away he heard a car pull up outside the house. He ran down the hall to look. It was a tatty black Morris. The door opened, Teddy Harris climbed out, and Taylor's heart sank like a stone.

Of course he was bound to get found out! Now it would be the police and heaven knows what. Harris would deny everything of course, his dad would get the sack, and he'd be done for shooting the kite. Then they'd be booted out of their house and it was all his fault.

The little old man stood in the living room with his wax anorak undone. The white fluff on his head was sticking straight up and he looked like a nutcase. He stared sadly at Taylor. His father towered over them both, his big hand wrapped round a mug of tea. He looked long and hard at his son as he came in.

Teddy Harris spread his arms. 'They've gone,' he said.

Taylor winced.

The old man passed his hand over his thin hair, making it stick up even more. 'I expect you knew – of course you did. Red kites! Nesting here in Hale Magna.' He shook his head. Taylor was embarrassed to see his eyes were damp. He glanced at his dad, who was watching him carefully.

'Egg thieves, by the look of it. There's signs of someone climbing up to the nest. Filthy … filthy…'

Taylor had expected Teddy to be cross, but instead he was standing there on the living-room carpet weeping. It made Taylor feel so sorry for him. He wanted to put his arm round his shoulders and make him feel better. He liked him; he wanted to be his friend. But he never could now.

'Anyway, they're gone,' Teddy went on. 'First the male disappeared – shot. Or poisoned.' He looked at Tom as if he thought he could say what had happened to the bird. But Tom just moved his hand and pulled a face.

'Now the nest's been raided and the female's flown.

First chance of kites nesting in England for thirty years – gone!'

'I'm sorry,' said Taylor.

Tom shook his head. 'It's a pity for the kites. But it doesn't surprise me, not at all. Folk round here don't like such things.'

Teddy turned to Tom. 'Not the sort of bird that's very popular with gamekeepers, Mr Mase, are they?'

Tom smiled wryly. What with Harris keeping him busy and Teddy sniffing around he hadn't had time to go and poke out that nest. He would have, though, if someone hadn't come along and done the job for him.

But Teddy obviously believed Tom was behind it. 'If it wasn't for you and your kind, those birds would be nesting far and wide by now,' he scolded.

Tom shrugged. 'As to that, I'd be quite happy for myself to see them nesting out there in one of my apple trees. But I have a job, you see. My boss – well, you'll know for yourself. Reg Harris is a fierce man when it comes to looking after his pheasants.'

'My nephew gave me his word that you'd leave the kites alone.'

Tom made no comment.

'And of course I know all about Reg,' snapped the old man. 'But we all have heads on our own shoulders. There are other jobs. We have to make our own decisions about such things.'

Tom scowled. 'I have a wife and son to keep. I don't see that I should have to lose my house and drag my son away from school and go looking for more work just because of some bird. This is our place.'

'Then where is the place for the kites, man?'

'The wild places …'

'But there *are* no wild places. I keep telling people: if the wild things are only to live in wild places, that's an end to them. We have to make our wild places all around us these days or not at all.'

Tom shrugged. What was to be done? He would have loved to be able to watch kites circling above the woodland of a morning. But it just wasn't practical and there was an end to it.

'There's another generation that may think differently,' said the old man.

He took out from under his coat a parcel wrapped in brown paper. 'Now, Taylor, I know you love the birds…'

'But so does my dad, really,' insisted Taylor. 'He does, don't you, Dad?'

But Tom was angry now. 'I have a job to do,' was all he'd say.

Teddy handed over the brown paper package. 'Go on, then – open it.'

Taylor glanced at his dad for permission. Tom nodded, and Taylor tore at the neat package. Under the brown paper was a layer of tissue paper. Under the tissue paper was a book – *Birds of the British Isles*. It was a big book, fat and heavy. No mere field guide, this, but a proper reference book.

Inside, on the thick paper, were the most beautiful paintings of birds Taylor had ever seen. They were full-page illustrations, each one covered by a layer of tissue paper to protect it. There were two or three pages of text to each bird that told you everything – where they lived, where and when they nested, how many eggs they laid, how they ate, bred and fed, everything you could hope to know.

But the glory was the pictures. On each page there was a big picture of the adults, male and female, coming in to land, taking off, feeding the young, perhaps. Down in a corner was another little drawing of the bird in flight and, in the other corner, of the egg.

'It's wonderful,' said Taylor, overawed.

'And that's not a reward for anything you may or may not have done,' said the old man. He held up a hand to stop the boy complaining. 'It's to encourage your interest in birds. But there's one condition.'

'What's that, sir?'

'No … more … eggs!'

Taylor looked at the heavy, expensive book in his hands. He thought of the treasure under his bed upstairs. He had loved collecting eggs, but the fact was he had poisoned it for himself by stealing from the kites.

'Yes, sir! It's a deal!'

Teddy smiled, and so did Tom. 'I'll see he keeps his word, Mr Harris. It's a lovely gift. And a deal's a deal, eh, Taylor?'

'Right, Dad. No more eggs!'

After Teddy had gone, the whole family sat around the dining room table to have a proper look. It was a wonder, that book. The price was marvellous for a start. There it was on the back flap – twelve guineas. It almost gave his mother a heart attack.

'It must be the most expensive thing in the house,' she groaned.

But it was worth it for the pictures. The robin *was* a robin, sitting on a twig watching you as you dug the garden. How many times had they all seen such a thing? The pheasant in his glory strutting over the cornfield stubble was so true – the way he held his head and peered from side to side.

'Wonderful, wonderful!' Tom kept saying. But he was less pleased when a slip of paper fell out from between the pages. It was a note from Teddy to Taylor.

'Please love what's inside the eggs more than the outside. And if you ever see or hear of kites again, let me know!' And there was his address in Taunton written on the top.

'Going behind my back,' complained Tom.

'But I could tell him, couldn't I?' begged Taylor

'You'll tell me first.'

Taylor scowled and turned the pages of the book to the birds of prey until he found what he wanted. His heart beat faster with fear.

There it was – the red kite.

The bird was standing on a tree, gazing out of the book with dark eyes. Under its claws was a fat young rabbit.

'Oh, you wicked, wicked villain!' cried his father. He pointed his finger at the bird and said, 'Bang!' And he winked at Taylor, as if he was just teasing, even though he really had killed a kite.

Down in one corner was the painting of the egg, a

beautiful chocolatey globe, just as Taylor remembered it. Just as it lay now under the hen in the coop in the garden … waiting to be discovered …

As soon as he thought about it Taylor's heart started thundering like a waterfall. What had he been thinking of? He'd forgotten all about it!

He had to go and get it at once.

'Where are you off to?' demanded his dad, as he slid off his chair and headed to the door.

'Won't be a sec.'

Taylor went out of the room and hared down the hall. As soon as they'd finished looking at the book his dad would go out to the back to feed his dogs, his mum would be in the kitchen most likely and they'd see him messing around with the hen run. He had to get that egg out and he only had a few minutes to do it.

He was going so fast he skidded on the grass and got his trousers covered in mud. Quick as a flash he opened the door to the hen run.

'Cheep, cheep, cheep!' A handful of tiny fluffy bodies bobbed under his hand. The hen had hatched her eggs. Taylor peered in.

It was dusk, he could hardly see a thing. The hen was sitting quietly on her nest. He slipped his hand carefully underneath her. He could feel the small, fluffy warm chicks squirming under his palm … and something else. It was small and hot and sticky and soft.

Gently he closed his hand and drew it out. The hen clucked and pecked at his knuckles. Kneeling on the grass before the coop, Taylor opened his hand to have a look.

The kite's egg had hatched.

The little thing lay on his palm flat on its stomach, wheezing. Its tiny sides fluttered – up and down, up and down, up and down. It seemed to be bleeding. But it was alive. It was a miracle. The egg had been crushed, but the chick inside was all right.

Taylor tucked his hand under the hen to make sure all the shells were gone. There was nothing there, but as he did it the kitchen light came on. Taylor thrust the chick into his trouser pocket, closed the door to the coop and ran bent double in the dark, before anyone could stop him.

He paused in the outhouse and scooped up a couple of fingerfuls of dog food, which he stuck in his other pocket. Then he braved the back door and the kitchen.

His mum was ironing; they were going out tonight. She knew at once he was up to something. 'Where've you been?' she demanded.

'… just went out to look at the new chicks.'

'Bit dark, isn't it? What are you up to?' demanded his mother suspiciously. She knew Taylor inside out.

Taylor grinned and ran upstairs.

The kite chick was bleeding from half a dozen places. It looked as though it had been attacked by the mother hen. First crushed, then pecked, but it was still alive. Taylor took some dog food in a pair of pincers and the chick gaped obediently. In went the dog food, and then more and more. When it was stuffed, the little thing fell over onto its great, fat, bald tummy, and went to sleep.

A kite chick. His kite chick. And he had saved it even though it was just by accident. If he hadn't climbed that tree his dad would have poked out the nest.

'And now there're twenty-four again,' whispered Taylor.

But what on earth was he going to do with it?

Six

Sitting on Alan's bed, Taylor gently removed the top off the shoe box on his lap. Alan looked doubtfully at the pathetic lump lying there. All he wanted to talk about was the wonderful book. Teddy had given him one, too, and taken the same promise.

Taylor leaned across and whispered, 'It's a red kite. I told you they were here! I rescued it!'

'No, it isn't. No, you didn't,' said Alan. A kite? It didn't even look like a bird. It was more like a blob of melted grease held together with scabs and rolled in fluff.

'Idiot, it's a chick. Harris ordered Dad to poke out the nest, so I went and got there first. It's the only survivor. I rescued it. It's a total SECRET!'

Alan goggled.

The chick peeped. Taylor took out the pincers and a blob of mincemeat he'd pinched from the larder at home. He began popping little shreds into the gaping beak. As he did it he told the story.

How he'd climbed the tree while no one was there. How he'd tucked them under the mother hen. How she'd pecked the other two chicks to death before he got back to them. Of course he didn't dare let his dad or anyone except Alan know that he was bringing up a real kite. And it was true … except that some of it was a whacking great pack of lies and he left bits out.

By this time Alan was mopping it all up. Taylor was a hero! He'd always known that, somehow. Taylor knew how to do things. He could clean a gun; he could fire a gun! He could gut a rabbit or snap its neck; he knew how to go ferreting, how to train dogs, how to dose sick pheasants and how to set traps for weasels, rabbits and anything else. Now he'd started rescuing endangered birds of prey. Of course!

If it had been the other way round, if Alan had been telling all this to Taylor, Taylor would never have believed a word of it. Alan was so excitable, if he told you anything you started to think he'd made it up almost at once. But Taylor was different. He never made things up. So when he did tell fibs, they were obviously true.

Alan leaped to his feet. 'We have to tell Teddy Harris!' he crowed.

'No!' Taylor grabbed his arm. 'We can NEVER tell ANYONE! I'll get arrested for robbing the nest.'

'But you *saved* them, Taylor.'

'Doesn't matter, I still robbed it. They'll say I should have reported Harris and my dad, and I couldn't do that, could I?'

'No, no ...'

'Dad would lose his job. We'd get chucked out of our house. Harris *owns* our house. It's a *total* secret.'

Alan frowned. But he knew what Harris was like. 'But what are we gonna *do* with it, Taylor?'

'We're gonna bring it up and release it into the wild.'

'*Wow!*'

'We're going to add it to the breeding population.'

'Yeah! *Wow!* Wow, Taylor, wow! WOW!'

'And I can't keep it at home so we have to keep it in your garage.'

'… oh yeah …'

They told Alan's mum and dad that it was a buzzard. They said that Taylor would get into trouble if his dad or Harris found out he was rearing vermin, so no one must ever know. Terry and Sylvia James were pleased. They'd never liked the egg hobby, which was why the collection had to be kept at Taylor's house. They loved wildlife and they hated the hard line Harris took in the management of the woods.

Of course the boys could keep the buzzard in the garage. Of course they wouldn't say a word. They were only too pleased to see the boys conserving wildlife – whatever they could do to help!

'A buzzard, eh? Harris would foam at the mouth!' exclaimed Sylvia James. Alan gave Taylor a big, knowing wink. Taylor winked back, but he had to try hard not to giggle. He felt so pleased with himself for fooling everyone.

The garage wasn't the perfect place for a young kite to grow up. It was damp and cold, it smelt of petrol and paint, and there were dark oil stains spreading over the concrete floor. But at least Taylor's dad and Harris would never see it.

The boys cadged half a pound of cotton wool off Alan's mum and made a special deluxe nest, with a little moss on the inside to make the chick feel at home. It was important to keep the chick warm until it got a bit bigger and grew a few feathers. Taylor showed Alan how to chop the meat up fine and they fed the chick till it could take no more, and it keeled over backwards and fell asleep.

They both stood and peered down at the peacefully sleeping baby bird.

It looked ridiculous. Was this really the fabulous kite?

Alan gulped and glanced nervously at Taylor. 'I bet it's really totally illegal to keep wild kites, isn't it, Taylor?'

'Nah!'

'I bet it is.'

'Maybe.'

One minute Alan was jigging round the garage cackling in glee, the next he was chewing his fingernails and fretting. Taylor didn't blame him. He was scared silly himself. Of course it was illegal! The kite should be with the RSPB or something like that. He was terrified Alan would change his mind and tell him to take the bird away.

'It won't be for long,' he told his friend. 'Just a couple of weeks until it gets old enough to keep outside. Then we'll find one of those old sheds in the woods that no one uses any more.'

'How long before it learns to fly?' whispered Alan. They were both speaking in hushed voices, partly because the chick was asleep, partly because they were talking crime.

'Dunno.'

They gazed at the chick. A kite – one of only twenty-odd left!

'It must be worth thousands and thousands of pounds,' said Alan.

The boys gulped.

Suddenly Taylor began to giggle.

'What?'

'Look at it … look at it …'

The chick was lying on its back against a big puff of cotton wool, with its flabby little beak in the air and its bald little wings folded over its tum.

'It looks like someone's gran!' giggled Taylor. He was right. It looked just like a bald, bare, ancient old lady gone to sleep in a chair. And it was just a baby, it was so funny …

They both began to laugh. Alan plumped the cotton wool up under its head. Taylor tried to rearrange its wings so they were folded behind its head, but the little chick woke up, tried to stand up and fell on its front, where it promptly stuck up its bottom and …

'It pooed! It pooed!' whooped Alan.

Taylor got a bit of cotton wool and wiped it. 'Wipe your granny's bum,' said Alan, and they both started hooting again. It was really hysterical.

Then at last, when the laughter died down, they folded the cotton wool ever so carefully over the top of the chick, and tiptoed out.

The best bit about keeping the chick at Alan's was that Taylor didn't have to worry about getting found out. The worst bit was he had to go home while Alan got on with the important work of caring for it. He spent ages each evening with the chick squatting on his hand, talking to it and feeding it while Taylor was stuck at home. Taylor was as jealous as a cat.

A few days after it hatched, the ugly black pads on the sides of the chick's head opened and a pair of dangerous yellow eyes looked out. Fed on a diet of minced vermin, the kite was growing like a balloon full of water. Its bottom spread out and it grew a pile of fluff on top of its head. It was soon covered in white down, from which a black, bald face peered greedily.

It looked daft.

'It looks like a Teddy Boy in rompers,' exclaimed Alan's mother.

For a few days the chick was called Ted after Teddy Harris. But then the boys decided that the chick was female. Really they had no idea what sex it was, but it was much funnier thinking it was a girl because it was so ugly. So they christened her Teresa.

Teresa grew so fast Alan claimed someone was sneaking in at night and pumping her up through her bottom. Her beak, which was quite soft at first, grew hard and sharp. Not only that, but she didn't see any difference between fingers and food. After having their fingers sliced two or three times Taylor and Alan got themselves a pair of long tweezers to pop the meat down her ever-open throat.

The chick was soon on her feet, and looking dafter than ever. Her feet were floppy, sausagey sorts of things, and far too big, as if she'd been given a spare pair by an old turkey that didn't fit. At first she just crouched there, shivering on them. But she soon learned to go places. Whenever Taylor or Alan opened the door to the garage, she would crawl out of her box and stagger up and down the shelf, peering down at them and screaming for food.

In another couple of weeks she could hold her meat and rip it up for herself. The boys were able to leave food in her nest with her while they were at school, which was a relief. It had been a real chore, chopping food up and stuffing it down her beak four times a day. Now, she could eat whenever she wanted and she started growing more quickly than ever.

For a while, as Teresa got fatter and fatter, she looked more and more silly. She grew round. She kept falling over her feet onto her tummy, which stuck out like an orange, and then she couldn't get back up. She seemed too big. She sat in her box like a huge, overweight, wobbly toy.

They had just about decided that they were overfeeding her when, almost overnight, she began to turn into a proper bird.

It was as though the true bird shape was hidden inside that baby fat all along. The two little sticks of skin on her sides turned into wings, prickly with new feathers. Her head narrowed, her beak got longer and even sharper and turned yellow at the base. And through the down that covered her from head to foot, the brownish-red plumage of the adult bird began to show.

Taylor watched the feathers grow, and worried. Soon, it would be obvious that this was no buzzard and they'd have to hide her in the woods. Alan was quite looking forward to that, but for Taylor it was different. There were several old sheds scattered about the woods where the keepers hardly ever went. Hardly ever – but once in a while. Once she was in the woods, there was a chance Teresa would be discovered.

Taylor and Alan had turned into a right pair of little mothers. They were always worrying. Was Teresa warm enough, was Teresa was getting enough to eat, or getting too much to eat – was it the right sort of food in the first place?

'Heaven help your children, you're a pair of fusspots!' exclaimed Alan's mother one day, when she found them arguing over whether Teresa should have a hot-water bottle at night.

The biggest worry was Smiley, Alan's big black and white tom cat. Smiley was a great thug of a cat, with a neck like a log, shredded ears, a lumpy, manky coat and a faceful of scars. Half the kittens in the village were fathered by Smiley, and there wasn't a cat in five miles who didn't know and fear him. He was also a famous hunter. The front garden was a death trap to wildlife. If he got into a hen run, it was a massacre. He'd take on a cockerel twice his size if he had the chance, and win.

Smiley, of course, had noticed the nice, warm, birdy smells coming from the garage. He miaowed until he grew hoarse, but no one let him in. He spent hours every day sitting outside the door listening to the noises inside and sniffing at the air, waiting for his chance. Taylor and Alan always made sure they pulled the door to, but the lock was old and one day it happened. The lock slipped as they walked out and neither of them noticed it.

Smiley did. As soon as he saw the open door, he pressed his belly close to the ground and slid in through the crack – the ambition of weeks of waiting!

Once inside, Smiley wasted no time in jumping up onto the shelf. He landed with a heavy thud and sniffed the box. Ah! Just as he'd thought. There was a young fledgling in there. The cheek of it! But he'd soon put a stop to this.

Smiley began batting at the box with his paw to start the fun.

Teresa, who had been asleep inside, awoke at once and naturally thought it must be feeding time. With a pleased squawk she sat up and stuck her head over the top.

The young kite had by this time grown a long, powerful, hooked beak. A fringe of tatty, half-grown feathers covered her head, which made her look like an elderly thug on the lookout for someone to mug.

Smiley started slightly when he saw this dreadful face pop out of the box. Then he licked his lips and sneered. Okay, so the bird was a big one. That just made it all the more fun.

He fixed his deadly gaze on the bird and began lightly treading the ground with his forepaws, ready to leap.

The question that was on Teresa's mind – the question that was always on Teresa's mind – was, where's dinner? Why else should she be woken up? She looked about expectantly. But, what was this? She didn't understand. Alan and Taylor weren't even there; there was only some odd-looking black and white thing. That was no use.

Oh, well. She sighed, and was about to flop in the box and go back to sleep – but wait. The black and white thing! Well, what else could it be? Teresa had no idea about cats. Admittedly she had never seen a dinner quite like this one before. The colours were a bit odd and it was still moving. But what else could it be?

Smiley was obviously a tasty titbit that Taylor and Alan had thoughtfully left for her. And look at the size of it! This was no mere dinner. This was a feast!

Teresa, who had a lot of character but not all that much brain, opened her beak wide and gave a squawk of happiness. The feathers on the back of her head lifted in delight. She drew her head back, and just as Smiley launched into his deadly 'bye bye birdy' jump, she lunged forward with her full weight behind that hard, sharp beak.

And scored a direct hit right up the cat's ear hole.

There was an unearthly screech. Smiley shot off the shelf like something on rocket fuel, rushed twice around the garage and hid, trembling with shock, behind a stack of oil and paint cans in a corner.

Teresa was as surprised as the cat. She jumped back, tipped out of her box and fell sideways off the shelf. She did flap, quite hard, but all she did was spiral down like a whirligig. Her bottom slapped against the cold concrete with a good hard smack.

She quacked in pain. She got up and staggered twice around the garage before she realised that her beloved box – home, dinner-table and bed – was miles away and hopelessly out of reach. Now it was Teresa's turn to panic. She began running round and round in circles looking for somewhere to hide. She went several times right round the garage, grunting and honking in despair, before she realised there was only one place – the very same stack of cans where Smiley was hiding.

She made straight for it.

Smiley had been peeking nervously out to see what this dangerous bird was up to. He saw with alarm that it had come down off the shelf and was now rushing round the garage looking for him, uttering ferocious war cries. Then, horror! The cat-eating bird suddenly homed in and came honking round behind the tins. Smiley opened his jaw and screamed in fright.

So did Teresa.

Both animals did an about-turn and hurtled out from behind the paint cans. Teresa ran straight into the wall, smack! Smiley made for the door, but just at that second, Taylor and Alan, who had heard the racket from outside, burst into the garage. One glance told them everything. There was the empty box, there was the cat, staring at them guiltily from the floor. Their worst nightmare had come true. Smiley had eaten Teresa!

With terrible howls of grief and rage, both boys lunged at the cat.

Smiley took one look at them, turned, and fled back into the garage, straight at Teresa, who was watching with a bruised beak from the wall.

When she saw the cat coming back at her, Teresa did what came naturally to her. She tripped up over her own feet and fell flat on her fat tummy, with a loud quack. But all Smiley saw was yet another ear-stabbing lunge coming right at him. The cat-eating bird was coming in for the kill!

All directions were blocked, so Smiley did the only thing left; he tried to climb the wall and hide on the ceiling. But panic and gravity foiled him and he fell with a thud onto the shelf, straight into Teresa's box. The box bounced with his weight and fell like a brick to the floor, with Smiley still in it.

Teresa was outraged. She'd been terrified before, but now that Taylor and Alan were there she was suddenly full of courage. Life was one thing; the box was another. Screaming with outrage she rushed forward to save her box.

Smiley stuck his tail in the air, stood on tiptoes and hissed like a gas attack. On one side, the cat-eating monster came bounding at him, its horrid feet slapping unpleasantly on the concrete floor. On the other, the two boys, howling like mad dogs, reached out with furious hands …

He flattened himself to the floor and ran, writhing between Taylor and Alan's legs, more like an eel than a cat. He went through the door and shot across the lawn as if he'd been fired out of a shotgun. He was out of the garden and across two more before next door's dog, who was sleeping on the lawn, even had a chance to bark.

Teresa was unhurt by her adventure, but felt very, very hungry after all that exercise. They gave her a jay as a reward and got very excited about her ferocity. She hadn't even grown her feathers and here she was, trying to eat cats! But really, Teresa had had a narrow escape. If she hadn't struck at a lucky moment, Smiley would certainly have killed her.

As for Smiley, he wasn't to know that. He never went in the garage for the rest of his life in case the terrible bird with the beak might be there, waiting for a go at his other ear.

Seven

As she grew up, Teresa returned all the affection Taylor and Alan gave her. She would come when they called her. She liked to play with blobs of meat and bits of fur, and chased dead birds tied to a piece of string across the floor. She loved being stroked. She was more like a pet, a puppy or a kitten, than a wild bird. The boys affectionately started to call her puss when they rubbed her neck and she butted their hands for more strokes.

Meanwhile, those long red feathers were shooting through. It was only a matter of time before Alan's mum or dad started wondering what sort of a buzzard it was that had such a long, forked tail. Taylor worried, but didn't do anything yet. Teresa had been safe in the garage. He and Alan were scared to put her in one of the old huts in the woods, where anything could happen to her while they were at school.

Then all that changed.

One day in the playground at school a boy came up to Taylor and asked him if it was true that he and Alan had a red kite in a cardboard box at home.

Taylor froze. He rolled his eyes as if such a thing was ridiculous.

'Who told you that?'

'Alan.'

'A kite,' scoffed Taylor. 'There aren't any kites round here. They're practically extinct.'

'He said …'

'He's just a kid! You don't want to believe what he tells you. It's a buzzard. It was hard enough getting a buzzard.' Taylor sneered, but his heart was going like a hamster in a wheel. The boy shrugged and started asking what they fed it with, and Taylor tried to explain it was a secret because of Harris and his dad. But it was too late. The news would be right round the school by the end of the day.

'You weren't even supposed to say we had a buzzard and now you've told everyone it's a kite. You're dead!' exclaimed Taylor when he got Alan on his own, on the way home. He pushed the smaller boy roughly into a hedge.

'I didn't, I didn't tell anyone!'

'You're a liar!' Taylor was so angry he clenched his fists and swung at Alan. He got him on the shoulder.

Alan's eyes filled with tears. 'I didn't mean to, I was just…'

'Did you know that Dave Cameron's dad is a policeman, and he's best friends with Sammy? I expect Dave Cameron is telling his dad RIGHT NOW that YOU'VE got an illegal red kite in your garage. I expect the police'll be round your house tonight. Your dad's gonna be ARRESTED. And you, you'll get taken away!'

Alan turned white.

'I'll tell 'em about you!' he howled. 'I'll tell 'em how you STOLE the eggs because they were worth money and your dad'll get SACKED and you'll get thrown out of your HOUSE!'

And it was all true! Taylor swung again, red with fury. He grazed Alan on the cheek. Alan fell over and scratched his knees on the tarmac and Taylor ran, not from fright but to hide his tears. He pounded down the road and leapt over the fence into the woodland. He heard Alan shouting, 'Taylor! Taylor!' behind him, but he didn't stop. He ran deep into the trees. When he was sure Alan wasn't following and he was really alone, he grabbed a stick and began to beat the bushes, until he suddenly began to cry.

It was all horrible! Such a mess. The kite was evidence, just sitting there waiting to be discovered.

After his tea, Taylor moped around in his bedroom. He wasn't cross any more, just scared. He hated leaving Teresa at Alan's house. It was his kite, after all.

He thought of Alan sitting there worrying. What would he do? He never did anything without Taylor. But suppose he did, suppose he decided to get rid of her? He was just a kid. He might let her go in the bushes, where another cat or a dog would get her.

'He'd better not,' snarled Taylor to himself. He began pacing round the bedroom, angry again. He punched the pillow viciously. Telling was bad enough but' if he did anything to the kite …

Then Taylor thought of poor Alan sitting round there on his own, chewing his nails and waiting for the police to knock at the door and drag the whole family away and lock them up. Every time he heard the phone ring or a knock at the door, he'd be jumping up to hide!

Taylor began to chuckle. Poor old Alan, stuck on his

own with the kite. He wouldn't have a clue what to do with it!

Taylor was quite right.

On his own, with a highly illegal bird of prey sitting in the garage and the gossip he had himself started running around the village, Alan was terrified. It was just a matter of time before the police came round to arrest his whole family!

Without Taylor to tell him whether his ideas were good ones or bad ones, Alan felt lost. He thought about putting Teresa in a cardboard box and letting her go in the woods, but she'd get eaten by a fox or something, and then he'd be in worse trouble than ever. He fed the bird and miserably stroked her neck. She butted his hand with her head, but he didn't have the heart to play. After his tea he went upstairs and lay down on his bed. He'd never felt so miserable in his life. If only Taylor would come back!

That's when there was a ferocious hammering at the door.

Alan leapt to his feet. It was them! The police, come for him. Downstairs he heard his poor innocent mother run down the hall to answer it.

The pounding on the door began again. In desperation, Alan did what he always did when he was in deep trouble. He dived to the floor and hid under his bed.

Downstairs, Mrs James was surprised to see Taylor standing at the front door with a cardboard box under his arm.

'Taylor! Is that your new knock? I thought it must be the police or something.'

'That's what you were meant to think,' growled Taylor.

She peered into the box. 'And what on earth are you going to do with those?' she wanted to know.

Under the bed, Alan cringed and shivered as the floor creaked outside his room. From the weight of a huge constable, no doubt.

Biting back his tears, he peered out from under the covers.

The door swung open and in came – oh horror! A pair of huge black boots! Policeman's boots! And above them the dark blue trousers!

It was all true. They'd come for him, just as Taylor had said they would. His life was over.

Alan whimpered and held his breath.

'Please let them go away, please God, please don't let them find me please…'

The policeman strode into the room, his huge legs swinging like pendulums. The way he walked he must be about twenty feet high! What bad luck – getting taken away was bad enough – but it *had* to be a giant policeman who came for him. Alan was gibbering. And then behind the policeman, smaller feet. Taylor! They had Taylor and now they had him! All was lost!

Taylor's face appeared under the bed. 'You can come out now,' he said.

Alan crawled out, almost weeping with terror. But, what was this? Where had the policeman gone? All that was left of him was his boots and the last foot or so of his legs. Taylor was holding in his hand two sticks with boots stuck on the bottom and with blue cloth wrapped round them.

'You…'

Taylor began to laugh.

'But how did you *know*, Taylor? How *did* you know? How did you know I'd be *under* there, Taylor? Huh? How did you? How did you *know* I'd be under my bed, Taylor?'

'You *always* hide under your bed,' roared Taylor.

'Do I?'

'Every time. Always, always, always … Oh, *look* at your *face!*'

The two boys fell about on the bed and rolled from side to side laughing. It was ten minutes before they stopped giggling and were able to go down and have a look at Teresa.

Taylor was relieved to discover the kite still there. At least Alan hadn't tried to get rid of her. He sat down next to her box on the shelf and tickled her behind the head. The kite shut her eyes and pushed against him, like a cat.

'Puss, puss, puss,' teased Taylor. 'Who's a lovely puss?'

'I'm sorry,' said Alan. 'I'm really sorry. I was stupid.'

'Correction … you *are* stupid,' said Taylor.

'What we gonna do? Do you *really* think Dave Cameron's dad'll come round if he finds out about it?'

'You'd better hope he *doesn't* find out about it.'

'And you. You'd better hope, too,' said Alan, fighting back.

'Anyway, I'm gonna move her,' said Taylor. 'It's time anyway; she's getting her feathers. She can't stay here now.'

'Can I come?'

'You'll tell everyone where she's hidden and they'll come and get her.'

'I won't!'

'That's what you said last time.'

'I won't, though. Go on, Taylor, I've learned my lesson.'

'You're a blabbermouth.'

'Oh, please, Taylor, please, Taylor, PLEASE, please let me come … Go on. Please? PLEASE!'

'Huh. Maybe. Well, let's get her into this box anyway.'

Taylor pushed his hand behind Teresa's tail and she obediently stepped back. Her sharp talons dug hard into his sleeve.

'Ow!'

Alan grinned proudly. 'Strong, ain't she?'

Taylor lifted his arm with the bird on through the air towards the cardboard box. But he moved too quickly and Teresa lost her balance. She opened her wings, and for the first time ever, she beat at the air.

They had seen her stretch her wings before, but this was different. Suddenly the garage was filled with wind. Taylor opened his mouth and cried out in pain as the fierce talons bit through his jacket, his jumper and his shirt, right into his flesh. He held the bird up high to avoid the huge wings, and she lowered her head and drove the air. For a moment they really thought she would lift off. Dust and litter rose from the floor. Dear old Teresa, with her batty haircut and dopey eyes and big silly beak, was transformed. Suddenly that dark eye looked merciless, the beak deadly.

Then she closed her wings, blinked and squawked in surprise. She looked anxiously at Taylor and Alan to make sure it was all right, as if to say, 'Wow! Did you see that? Was that *me*?'

She could catch the wind.

'She'll be able to fly soon,' realised Alan. 'Then we'll have to let her go. Won't we? Won't we, Taylor? Huh?'

But they both loved her far too much to want to see her go.

They carried Teresa in a cardboard box wedged onto the carrier at the back of Taylor's bike. He rode as carefully as he could, but he heard her skidding and shuffling inside the whole time. When they got to the woods, they hid their bikes in the bushes, jumped the fence, and made their way to her new home.

Taylor had been keeping an eye out, and he had just the place. It was only a little shed, all crooked and half rotted, but it was tucked well away from the usual paths his father and Old John took. There had been rearing coops in the same clearing a few years ago, but they had been moved on and since the shed was old it had been left behind.

There were a number of old sheds, rotting and falling to bits in the woods, but the good thing about this one was that his father had repaired the roof. There was a good shoot nearby, and sometimes in the autumn the shed was called out of retirement to store the bodies, or cartridges. So the shed was both unused and dry – just right.

At least, it had seemed just right when he'd last checked it out. Now, standing among the brambles that were growing up around it, it looked horrible.

'It's titchy!' complained Alan. Taylor shrugged.

'And there's no window.'

'Well, what do you want, people peering in all day? Oh, look there's a red kite in there, I wonder how it got there?'

'But she'll be in the dark all day.'

'Well, she wouldn't have been in the dark all day if you hadn't blabbermouthed, blabbermouth!'

But Alan was right. The shed was so small Teresa wouldn't even be able to spread her wings, which were four feet across already. And it was dark. She'd be locked up all day like a battery chicken in a box.

Teresa stepped awkwardly off Taylor's fist onto the dirty floor. Her wonderful tail trailed in the dust and muck.

'She needs a perch, we'll have to make her a perch,' said Taylor. They stroked and petted her, but when they stood up she stared anxiously up at them and began to scream. It was an awful noise, 'Kwaaa, kwaaa, kwaa', over and over again, because she was upset about being stuck on the ground and didn't understand what was going on.

They left some carrion for her, but when they backed out of the door she ran towards them and screamed, begging them not to leave her here.

'Do you think the vermin can get in? Weasels and stoats and rats, I mean?' asked Alan anxiously.

'If she can deal with Smiley she can handle a weasel, easy!' said Taylor. But he wasn't really sure. They spent another half an hour blocking up the holes around the bottom of the shed, where the long wet grass had rotted the wood. From inside Teresa kept up her awful yells, kwaa kwaa, kwaa, over and over again.

'If she carries on like that Harris or your dad'll hear her and that'll be it.'

'Oh, stop moaning, will you?' snapped Taylor. 'There's nowhere else for her. She'll shut up when she's left alone, it's just us hanging around all the time.'

At last there was nothing more they could do. They went inside one more time to comfort her, but seeing them leave again just upset her more than ever. They could hear her angry, urgent calls following them for ten minutes or more, kwaa, kwaa, help me, help me, as they pushed their way back through the hanging branches towards their bikes.

When he got home, Alan told his father that the 'buzzard' had grown up and that they'd let her go.

'Let her go?' exclaimed his father. 'But she can't fly yet!'

'She can, nearly. She makes a hell of a draught.'

Mr James was furious. After rearing the buzzard so carefully for so long, they'd suddenly let it go too soon. It would certainly be dead before the morning. But he didn't let his son see how cross he was. The boys had done it out of the best intentions. You'd have thought they'd be hanging on to the bird for too long, rather than letting it go too soon.

'You should have waited another week or two,' was all he said. Alan shrugged and went upstairs. And that was that.

And at school the next day, the boys spread the story. The buzzard had been let go. Now, no one but they knew that Teresa was still in captivity.

The boys promised themselves they'd see Teresa at least twice a day, in the morning before school and again in the evening. But the morning visits proved impossible. The hut was hidden too far away. Sometimes they got there straight after school, and again after tea. But too often, Teresa was locked away in the hut all day and all night alone and only got to go outside once a day.

At first she called to them when she heard them coming through the bushes, which scared them to bits, since it meant she would call out in the same way if she heard other people passing by, Tom or Harris, for instance. But one day they opened the door to find her huddled on the floor, crouching as far away as possible from them. It took them ages to tempt her to take her food and sit on their fists. Something must have happened when she was left alone. Perhaps a fox had visited, or a poacher passing by had heard her and beaten on the sides of the shed.

Each day when they carried her outside, she sat up straight and stared at the trees, blinking at the bright light. She sat nervously on Taylor's fist and when he lifted it up high to make her beat her wings, she made the leaves shake and the grass bend. She wasn't growing so fast now. She was almost as big as she was going to get, and all her growing was concentrated on her wings and on her feathers. She was preparing to fly.

In the wild, the kite would have been flying already, but trapped all day in the narrow shed, she had no chance to exercise her wings except for an hour or two each day, when the boys visited her. Even so, each day when Alan and Taylor perched her on their hands and held her up, the wind under her wings grew stronger.

They knew it had to happen, but when it came it took them completely by surprise.

One day, as Alan was holding her high to let her beat, she gripped his arm so hard that he gently touched her foot, and Teresa let go. Beneath her, the wind was suddenly free. Before either she or the boys knew what was happening, the kite began to rise up towards the canopy.

'Hey!' It was unbelievable. Teresa was a great big lump; she weighed a ton on your arm. But here she was, suddenly lighter than the air, floating …

'Hey! Hey! Teresa!' The two boys ran about on the ground as the kite kicked at the air and soared up and flapped and staggered on the wind.

'Come on, girl!' yelled Taylor, half overjoyed to see her fly, half terrified she was going. The kite wobbled in the air. She flapped up and down, half hovering, half flying. Then she suddenly grabbed the wind properly with her wings, did two powerful flaps and disappeared beyond the trees.

Taylor and Alan stared dumbfounded at the place where she had been. Was that it? Was it over, suddenly like that? The branches swayed in the wind, the leaves sighed. There was no sign of the kite.

Alan started running about under the trees, shouting, 'Teresa! Teresa!' There was no answering call. The kite had totally vanished. But Taylor stood still and sighed deeply. It was over ... and he was relieved. No more worry about getting caught. No more worry about the kite being his responsibility. He'd owed the kite something but now he'd paid her back. It was quits.

Taylor sat down on the floor at the shed door and watched Alan running up and down, shouting. It had been a warm day. Behind him, the air in the shed was hot, far too hot to keep any kind of animal in, he realised.

It was a good thing she had gone.

Teresa was free. And so was he.

Above the canopy, there was a call. 'Hi-hi-heea! Hi-hi-heea!' Alan screamed in pleasure. And there she was, circling in the air above them, hovering all wobbly. Alan held his arm up and Teresa swooped down, making a bid to land but missing and flapping back up. Staring at the outstretched arm, she tried again, and landed with a thud. Alan yelped in pain where she gripped his arm.

'Wow, Taylor, wow, Taylor! She's come *back*. She's come back!'

'Wow!'

'YEAH!' grinned Alan. It was like a miracle. She'd come back!

Taylor swallowed down his disappointment and ran over to pet her. 'Gorgeous puss,' he said. He stroked her head and she butted at his hand like a cat.

'Poor puss!' exclaimed Alan. 'Was it too high for oo? Alan laughed happily. She'd had the wind to ride and she'd chosen to stay and live in the hot, smelly, little hut, just because of them.

'Gorgeous,' said Alan.

'Gorgeous!' echoed Taylor. And he grinned suddenly, because she was gorgeous, after all. She loved them. She was the most beautiful thing in the world and she was theirs.

Eight

'It's the sock monster!'

'Sock head!'

'She looks ridiculous. Look ... *look* at her!'

The kite stood on her perch, perfectly still. They'd fooled her into thinking it was night time by putting one of Taylor's old socks over her head. The boys had never seen anything so funny.

'Isn't she *stupid*!'

'Poor old puss. The sock goes on your *foot*, not on your head!'

'Gas alert – gas alert – gas alert!'

'The RSPCA could get you for this, Taylor.'

'And you!'

'It's *your* sock. We'll be able to tell where she is a mile off now by the cheesy stink.'

'The rare sock-headed kite!'

'The very rare cheesy-headed kite!'

'Stink-hawk! Kills its prey at twenty yards by smell alone!'

'Arrgh! It's got me!'

The sock wasn't because they wanted to torment Teresa. They were still planning on letting her, go. But ... not quite yet. First she had to get her flying practice.

Taylor had found an old book on falconry at home. As soon as they saw it, the boys knew exactly what to do next.

They pored over it. It told you everything about keeping birds of prey. Of course Teresa was a kite, and kites were more scavengers than hunters. But that was just a detail.

'We can teach her to *hunt*!' exclaimed Taylor in ecstasy.

Since Teresa had no real parents, they had to stand in. It was their duty to teach her! She could catch rabbits for them, maybe even hares!

'Wow, Taylor! WOW!'

When falconers took their birds out in daylight, they fitted little hoods neatly over their heads until it was time to fly. In the dark, the birds stayed still and were easy to handle. The hoods in the book were made of leather, neatly sewn, sometimes with a cluster of bright feathers on the top. The best the boys could manage was an old sock.

'Here, look.' Alan found a pheasant's feather on the floor. He stuck it on top of Teresa's head. Teresa looked worse than ever. The two boys howled. Teresa shuffled unhappily on her perch.

'Here, we'd better stop,' said Taylor suddenly. The really important thing was to keep her trust. That's what the book said. And here they were making a fool of her.

'Let's get going.'

Taylor put his hand under her tail feathers, and Teresa stepped backwards onto his arm. When he moved, the bird cried out in the darkness and beat her wings three or four times to keep her balance. The wing struck Alan on the shoulder and both bird and boy cried out.

'Careful!' yelled Taylor angrily, even though it was his fault. Teresa peered blindly this way and that, fluffed up her feathers and hunched down. Taylor could feet the steely grip of her talons biting into his arm.

'Got the line?'

Alan pulled a ball of string out of his pocket. One end of this was tied to a loop on Teresa's leg. They planned on flying her round and round their heads, like an aeroplane on a string.

The boys stepped out of the hut into the dappled air. Teresa rose on Taylor's wrist and listened to the wind moving the trees.

'She weighs a ton,' complained Taylor.

They stepped along the footpath, peering like outlaws. They were. This was Harris's land. The boys were planning to teach the bird to hunt his rabbits.

In other words, they were going poaching.

Taylor supported his arm by propping it up with the other one, but even like that the weight of the great bird was too much. Alan offered to carry her but Taylor sneered. If she was heavy for him, Alan would be useless. In the end Alan helped prop up the aching arm. Stuck together like this, they pushed their way past the overhanging branches.

What with watching their step, walking so close together, brushing the twigs and branches away so they didn't hit Teresa, it had to happen. Taylor's foot found a root and he tripped.

It was disaster. As he fell Teresa leapt off his arm and tried to take to the air, but she was tied to him and he flung her to the ground. There was a desperate tangle of boys and bird. Taylor fell heavily on his shoulder, Teresa crashed to the ground and leapt to her feet, hurt, blind and shocked. She tried to hop away, but the string around her foot entangled her. She screamed terribly in panic and rage.

Without thinking, Alan grabbed her by the neck, hard. 'Shut her up, shut her up,' he hissed. He squeezed too hard. Teresa flapped desperately and opened her mouth.

'Not so hard, you idiot!' yelled Taylor.

It took them ages to sort it out – to calm her down, to untangle the string. Teresa was hurt, scared and angry. They had a hot, whispered argument about whose fault it was before they carried on. But now Teresa was scared of the moving darkness. At the smallest jolt she reared up and flapped. Taylor was angry because she was making such a fuss, although he knew it was his fault.

Finally, he just tucked her under his arm. He didn't really like it. The books said the birds should always be perched on your fist or arm. Now, she was no better than a chicken going to market. But at least they were able to move.

They made for one of the clearings where the pheasants had been reared. The coops had been lifted months ago, and the young pheasants released. The clearing wasn't ideal; it wasn't big enough for the kite to really fly. But it was enclosed by trees, hidden from prying eyes, and it would have to do.

Teresa sat under Taylor's arm with her mouth open, panting slightly. Sick of the weight, Taylor carefully perched her on an old log lying on the ground. She stood up tall, very still. Gently, Taylor eased the sock over her head.

As soon as the sock was off, the kite screamed and struck a savage blow at his knuckles. It was like an axe. It smashed the skin off down to the bone and Taylor, with a shriek of pain, leapt backwards. At the same moment, Teresa leapt from the log into the air. Terrified that she was going to escape, but scared stiff of her, Alan lashed out at her and knocked her out of the air. The kite crashed hard onto the ground.

She clambered to her feet, bruised and winded. She stood panting, her mouth dry, staring around. She was terrified.

'Don't hurt her!'

'I didn't mean to!'

It was all going horribly wrong. Taylor was clutching his damaged hand under his arm, cursing with the pain of it. The skin hung off in a bloody ribbon. He glared at the kite, whom he was beginning to hate. He wanted to kick out at her, to hurt her back.

Teresa opened her wings and held them in a W. She took a little hop into the air.

'Get her!' yelled Taylor.

The two boys leapt. Teresa raised her wings and beat, but did not rise from the ground. Instead, she began to run, bounding and leaping over the grass like a tiny, strange old woman.

'Don't let her get into the bushes!' yelled Taylor.

Alan gave a great leap but Teresa slipped through his arms and went bounding and jumping into the bushes at the edge of the clearing.

Taylor groaned. But then he noticed the end of the string tied to Teresa's leg, snaking its way through the grass after her. Taylor jumped and caught the string in his hand. He pulled it until it caught the bird up short in the undergrowth. Then he began to reel it in. Teresa hadn't gone far, just a few feet under an elder bush. Now she came back out, backwards, hopping on one leg. She looked at Taylor and Alan and blinked. She opened her mouth. They could see the curled, narrow tongue inside, like the tongue of a griffon.

Taylor gave another tug. Teresa lifted a leg off the ground and hopped closer.

'Go on then … pick her up,' Taylor told Alan.

'Me?'

'I've got the string,' said Taylor.

Alan sighed, and crept up to the bird, who looked up at him, tilting her head. She looked much smaller on the ground on the end of a string than she had up in the air, or on Taylor's arm. Alan shielded his face with one arm and bent to grab the bird.

Teresa tried to jump away as he came, but the string tightened and she fell down on her side. Alan quickly scooped her up in his arms, but the kite lashed out. That vicious yellow beak went straight for his face. Alan turned away only just in time and the blow glanced off his forehead. He screamed in pain and fright and flung her away from him. Taylor yanked on the string as if he were fishing, and she crashed to the ground.

Alan clutched his head. It had only missed his eye by a couple of inches. Blood welled and flowed suddenly down his face.

'Ahh!' He clapped his hand to his head and stared at the blood. 'She's bloody dangerous, Taylor! She's deadly!'

It was stalemate. The kite sat in the grass. Taylor looked at the blood on Alan's face and scowled.

'She was tame when she was living with me,' scolded Alan. 'What's wrong with her?'

They stared at the kite and the kite stared back.

Alan said, 'I'm not going near her.'

'You wanted to help. You wanted to have a go,' accused Taylor.

'I don't care.'

There was a pause.

'If we come at her from two sides, one of us could grab her beak and then we'd be all right,' said Taylor.

There was another pause. Alan wiped the blood out of his eyes.

'I think we should let her go.'

'No! She's not ready.'

'You just want to keep her forever.'

'I don't!'

'You do.'

'We agreed she wasn't ready yet, remember? You're just scared.'

'I'm not!'

'Well, will you help me then?'

Alan pouted. 'We want something to catch her in. I'm not picking her up again, I'll tell you that.'

Taylor managed to find some old, half-rotted sacking in the long grass. With this wrapped round their hands they crept up on Teresa, who watched them nervously.

'Now!' shouted Taylor. They lunged. Taylor managed to grab the neck and squeezed hard. The yellow mouth opened and the bird gasped, wheezing for breath. 'Grab her beak, grab her beak!' yelled Taylor in a fright. Alan's hand hovered nervously a foot away. The bird struck down at the hand around her neck, but it was too close to her head.

'Hurry!'

Alan snatched at the beak, but then he pulled away with a yell. Teresa had bitten him; more blood. For a second Taylor hung onto her neck while Alan hopped around shaking his hand and yelling. Then he panicked and flung the bird away from him. The string caught her short and she thudded violently to the ground, a ball of screaming feathers and rage. Taylor danced around her, lunging and dipping at her, while she lunged back at him. This time he managed to get a decent grip around the bill.

Alan came running up and somehow they managed to force the sock over her head. By now, Teresa was so scared that even in darkness she screamed and lunged. It was horrible. Taylor got another deep cut on his forearm. They bundled her up inside the rotted sacking ... and at last the bird fell quiet.

'Falconry's hard, isn't it?' said Alan as they walked back with the angry weight of the bird under their arms.

Taylor was trying not to cry. Everything the book had told them not to do, they had done. The trust, the care they had built up, they had all been thrown away. It could take weeks before she trusted them again, maybe forever.

Back at the shed, he opened the sack and flung her inside. He felt sick of the whole thing. Teresa needed feeding but he wasn't going to do it. The kite was ungrateful. Let her starve a few days, he thought to himself. That'd teach her. See how she behaved then.

'What are we going to do now, Taylor?' asked Alan at his side. 'Shall we call Teddy Harris now? Shall we let her go?'

'She'd just get shot by my dad, wouldn't she?' Taylor was suddenly filled with hatred and rage at the kite. He slammed the door on her as hard as he could. He turned and walked away, raging at himself, at the bird, and at the whole filthy mess.

'But, Taylor ... what we gonna do?'

Taylor had no idea what to do. Keeping her in the shed was horrible. Training her was useless. He didn't dare tell Teddy Harris. He'd have to tell him how he got her. If they let her go she'd get shot.

He had come to love the bird but now she feared and hated him and he feared and hated her. Turning back to the shed, he suddenly stooped for a big stone and flung it hard at the door. Inside the kite exploded in fear.

'Taylor, stop it!' yelled Alan.

'Oh, shut up, you shut your mouth!'

Taylor burst into tears and ran off into the woods.

Alan followed slowly behind. He had no idea what was happening, or why. He was shocked. Taylor throwing a tantrum! Taylor, crying! It was awful.

Ten minutes later, Taylor was waiting for him at the fence where they jumped over onto the road. Both of them looked a right mess. He grinned at Alan and held out his hands with bloodstains on them.

'She puts up a good fight, doesn't she?'

'Yeah!' Alan smiled uncertainly. 'I'm glad I'm not a rabbit with her around!'

'Yeah!' Taylor nodded back down the path to the hut. 'I've been thinking. You're right. It's time to let her go. But not round here in case she gets shot. We'll go at the weekend. Take her on a picnic or something. Somewhere where there's no gamekeepers about.'

'Right, right. Brilliant.'

They stood and looked at each other. They really were a mess.

'Wow, wow, she really knows how to fight, doesn't she, Taylor? Look at the blood. Wow!'

'She'll be all right.'

'Yeah.'

Nine

As it happened, that Saturday a storm came. The trees heaved and swayed, the rain beat against the leaves and windows and sent rapids running down the roads. There was no chance of going out for a picnic or anything else that day.

Sunday dawned blue but not still. The clouds had passed on, but the wind still blew the trees and flattened the crops. The boys couldn't wait. They got their bikes, packed sandwiches, and told their mothers and fathers they were going for a bike ride.

Teresa had been alone in the shed with nothing to eat or drink since Friday, and she remembered their last meeting. She was savage. They danced around her trying to avoid her vicious blows, but they managed to get her wrapped up in a blanket without any serious injury. They tipped her into a cardboard box and quickly sellotaped the top up. With the box jammed tight onto the back of Taylor's bike, they finally set off.

It was hard work. Teresa was heavier this time. The wind buffeted them this way and that, and they got sick to death of it roaring in their ears and faces. Above, dark rain clouds began to blow past, and soon they had to find shelter under some trees. The rain was cold, the wind thrashed their wet hair in their eyes and slapped their wet clothes against them.

They took two soakings before they decided they'd had enough.

'Let's just let her go here,' demanded Alan.

'But it's too near ...'

'She can fly, can't she? She could fly as far in *one hour* as we could go in a whole day, I expect.'

Taylor had had enough, too. 'Anyway, her box is getting wet,' he said.

He took the cardboard box off the back of his bike and they walked away from the road, climbing a fence into the fields. The grass was soaking. The wind was trying to snatch the box out of their hands. They found a tree-high hedge at the edge of a patch of woodland where there was a bit of shelter, and Taylor put the box on the ground. Inside, Teresa scratched and thudded.

'Careful, then.'

They bent down. Taylor used his penknife to cut the Sellotape. Then they flicked open the flaps and stood back.

Teresa stuck her head out of the box.

She looked daft – like a chick again, with her feathers all over the place, only this time she looked sad, not funny. She peered this way and that. Then she started to pick irritably at the flaps of cardboard around her. She couldn't open her wings to help her flap up, so she tried to push the box over with her chest. Finally, she jumped out and tried to perch on the edge of the box, but the box fell over. She fell clumsily to the ground.

The wind tousled her feathers. Her beak was slightly agape. Above them in the trees the wind roared.

Teresa stared at them and screamed.

They had no idea if she was screaming in anger, or

sorrow. Perhaps she was just asking for food. Perhaps she knew they were deserting her and was begging them to keep her. Perhaps she just didn't understand.

'Shoo! Shoo!' yelled Taylor. All around them the rain began to fall again, hissing against the leaves. Teresa was getting wet. She blinked and shook her feathers.

'Maybe she wants to be friends,' suggested Alan. But Taylor had other ideas. Suddenly, to Alan's surprise, he made a rush at the bird, screaming and waving his arms as if he wanted to beat her to death. 'ARRRGH!' he yelled. 'SCRAM … BAD BIRD, BAD PUSS … GO ON! SCRAM! SCRAM!' Teresa jumped backwards and stared at him in amazement.

'Don't scare her…' began Alan.

'No, but that's what we have to do – scare her silly. See? So she knows people aren't friends. So she stays away from them. See? SCRAM, Teresa! Go on, then, yell at her, Al.'

Alan did as he was told. They both stood there waving their arms and shouting at her like a pair of idiots. Teresa took a couple of jumps back and then just stood there watching them curiously, with her head on one side. When they stopped she screamed at them again.

'I think she wants food,' said Alan. It broke his heart. She hadn't eaten for ages. They should have brought something for her.

Taylor broke off a stick from a bush and waggled it in the air, yelling. He threw it at her. 'Get away … bad puss … go … GO AWAY!' he screamed. He tore off another branch, Alan did the same and they threw them at the kite. One caught her on the chest and she screamed again, in pain this time.

At last Teresa jumped into the air. For a moment they thought she was flying at them and they lifted their hands to their faces, but she wheeled in the air and began to rise. She flew upwards in a half spiral, glancing down at the frightened boys, fighting against the wind. She paused in the air and took her bearings. Another couple of flaps and she reached the tree tops … and then the wind had her. It snatched at her – it was like watching a stick going over a weir. One second she was rising, pushing against the current. The next she was off like a bullet, shooting across the field. In just a few seconds, as the rain turned the sky grey, she had vanished from sight.

'There,' said Taylor. 'There. She's gone now.'

Alan sniffed.

'But I didn't want her to go, Taylor.'

'Well, she has. So just shut up.'

Ten

By the autumn the young pheasants were just right.

It had been a good year and they were everywhere, bursting out of the grass as you walked through a field, hopping off the road as a car turned a corner, hiding in hedges, running along the fences, kuk-kuk-kuking in the woods. The young males held their gaudy, red-daubed heads high as they paraded in the wheat stubble. The females crept unseen in brown and russet. They were all healthy and fat and lovely, and it was time to kill them.

'Common as sparrows,' said Tom Mase affectionately, watching yet another covey jump off the fence as he opened the door in the morning. They did havoc to his vegetable garden. Anne was always asking him to raise the fence, but he never got round to it. She scolded him, and said it was because he liked to watch them through the window.

'I get enough of pheasants the rest of the time without wanting them at home, too,' said Tom. But the fact was he loved them so much, he could forgive them anything, certainly a row or two of peas each year.

This year there was one special cock bird that Tom loved above all the others. Its plumage was a beautiful creamy white. Only at the rim of each feather was there a line of the normal russet, red and gold colouring.

Tom called him Dan the Man. He was a stunningly beautiful bird. Although he denied it, when Tom opened the curtains in the back room every morning it was in the secret hope he would see Dan the Man standing among the rows of peas. Dan the Man could have eaten the garden bald as far as Tom was concerned. He was hoping that he would get through the autumn and breed next year. Then the woods would be full of beautiful white, russet and gold birds stalking in the morning mists for all the years to come.

But to do that, Dan the Man had to survive the shoots.

The first few shoots were small affairs, just Harris, or Harris and a friend or two blasting happily away. 'Just to sharpen up the birds for the big day,' Harris claimed. The fact was he enjoyed being the only man with a gun surrounded by birds enough for thirty to shoot.

The big days came in the late autumn and winter.

The guns arrived on the Saturday night. Some came in big cars that glided up the gravel drive. Others came by train, and there was a steady coming and going of Harris's jag to pick them up. Harris was beside himself – one minute pleased and making awful jokes because the pheasants were good this year, the next screaming tantrums because he was worried that everything should go off smoothly.

The shoots were what it was all about: the gathering and hatching of eggs; the tending and rearing of the young birds; the slaughter of stoats and weasels, crows, jays, owls … and kites. It was all done so that when the guns came to visit, they would have plenty to do.

On Sunday morning, Tom got up at five. He woke his

wife and son up a quarter of an hour later with a cup of tea. Anne drank hers down, jumped straight out of bed and ran down to the big house to begin cutting sandwiches for the beaters and preparing lunch for the guns. She'd have her breakfast there. Tom cooked himself and Taylor a big fry-up, which they ate together, peering out at the front garden through the kitchen window. It was a moist, cool morning with a touch of frost, perfect for a long day outside.

'Did you find him?' asked Taylor. His dad had been out the back to try and catch Dan the Man, so he could lock him away and keep him safe for the day.

'Uh uh. He'll have to take his chances with the rest.' Tom pulled a face and shrugged. He dearly wanted that bird to live. He nodded at a pair of pheasants standing in the misty wet lawn before them. 'They're in the right place to stay safe.'

They put their dishes in the sink to soak, pulled on their boots and went out into the cold morning.

The first beat was at half past eight. Tom had the guns waiting behind the bushes outside a patch of woodland. The trees stood against a sky now clearing of mist and showing blue. The air smelt of fermenting leaves and earth. Taylor and Alan waited with the other beaters in a new pine plantation on the other side of the woodland.

The baby trees only came up to their waists. They stood quietly in the long, wet grass, already soaked to the knee with icy dew. There were about twenty men and boys armed with long sticks with a flap of stiff leather at the end.

Before them, in the bushes and the long grass, in among the little trees, the pheasants moved uneasily. So many people! So far, people had been good to the birds, but they were used only to Tom, Old John, Harris and a few others. Something was going on, but the pheasants had no idea what it was.

The whistle sounded. Someone shouted, 'Okay!' And the still of the morning was shattered.

The beaters made all the noise they could, shouting, bawling, banging and bashing at the undergrowth with their sticks. And out of every bush and from under every tree jumped a terrified pheasant.

The beaters made their way forward slowly. Before them the driven birds darted from grass clump to bush, from cover to cover, only to be scared off from each new hiding place. Within a few minutes they left the grass and ran into the cover of the woods. Still the beaters followed up behind them. Slowly the line of men and boys disappeared after the birds into the trees.

At last the pheasants came to the edge of the woods. Before them were scattered hedges and shrubs. Here they hesitated, unwilling to go out into the open. But the dreadful racket behind them closed in. The pheasants waited until the last possible moment before they left cover.

Only now, with nowhere left to hide, did the birds take to the air.

They flew up high. But always, always, always, they took to the air too late and could never fly fast enough or high enough. Only a few older birds from last year who knew what was coming doubled back into the woods, or made the extra effort to get the height that could carry them out of range. As they flew up, they were caught against the bright morning sky. The guns spoke.

The air was filled with a furious crack and thud and the whistle of lead shot. The handsome young birds, beating their way into the air, crumpled into an untidy ball of feathers and fell out of the sky. From where they waited in the woods, Taylor and Alan could smell the gunpowder on the wind and hear the bodies – tud tump tud – as they struck the ground. It went on and on and on.

At last the birds were all used up. At a whistle from Tom, the guns fell silent, and the beaters moved forward to collect the bag before moving on to the next shoot.

In the backs of the Land Rovers, the soft mounds of little corpses piled up. Tom's birds were healthy, flew high and fast and were not easy to hit. Even so the kill would number hundreds.

At lunch time, rows of trestle tables were set up spread with wine and delicacies for the guns. The keepers and beaters sat on the grass and ate bread and cheese.

Tom barely had time to sit down. He had to organise everything. But he made sure he found time to sit with Taylor and Alan and drink a cup of tea for a minute.

'So far, so good,' said Tom.

'What about Dan the Man?' asked Taylor.

'Haven't seen him so far,' answered his dad. He looked strained. His whole year's work would be judged on the success of this and a few other days like it.

The first beat of the afternoon was through a sloping patch of scrubland, knee high in grey grass and spiky gorse bushes. The beaters had to walk down the slope and into a wood, driving the birds before them. On the other side, the guns were waiting for the first troubled, peeking heads to appear through the bushes and in the stubble of a cornfield.

The whistle sounded; the beaters lifted their arms and yelled and walked slowly forward. From the bushes and out of the grass, Taylor could see the heads of the birds looking up – what's going on? Then the heads disappeared and there was a rustle of grass as they ran off towards the woods. But never to safety.

He was about halfway down the slope when he saw a couple of the men looking up to the sky. He followed their gaze. High in the sky, there was a great bird.

The wings hooked back, the buoyant, soaring flight – above all, the clear deep v-shape in the tail. Taylor would know it anywhere.

It was a red kite.

'Alan ... Alan ... look!'

Alan followed his finger into the air. Taylor could hear him let out a little groan of excitement. Could it really be?

'Is it her, Taylor?' he begged.

'It has to be, it *has* to be. There can't be two round here. It *must* be her. She survived. Wow! Look at her go!'

The kite was making sudden deep swoops to and fro, watching curiously what was going on so far below.

'It *must* be her! Look at her go, Taylor! Wow, Taylor. Look!'

Now the kite was floating, scanning the ground below. She was light, so quick and easy in the air. The two boys on the ground began to jump and whoop at one another because they'd done it. They really had saved her, and taken her back into the wild.

'TERESA! WA-HEY!'

And so maybe it was because she heard them call. She swooped a little lower. From the other side of the woods came a single shot, one of the guns firing off at an early pheasant. Taylor could hear someone shouting angrily at the man for firing before the signal. Lazily, the kite turned in the air and swooped down fifty feet closer. The beaters moved forward and began to enter the woodland. Someone yelled at Taylor and Alan for lingering.

'Come on, lads!'

Then on the other side of the woods the barrage started, a crackle of brittle thunder. The kite swooped again, so much lower, so much nearer. Then again. And again …

'Do you think…' began Alan.

'It'd be illegal,' said Taylor quickly. All the other beaters were in the woods now. The boys paused for a last glance. Teresa hung in the air, and then suddenly went into a dive. She was moving like a living plane in a long, low, fast swoop down towards the guns.

Without a word Taylor and Alan dropped their sticks and ran.

Harris was having a good day. He was being paid a great deal of money by the guns for the day's shooting. The birds were good, flying high and fast, and there were plenty of them. He had just blasted a fine male pheasant out of the air. He turned his gun onto another soaring out of the woods. It was right up high, it was a difficult shot, but he got it bang to rights. It puffed feathers up in the air and fell.

Harris beamed. 'A one and a two,' he said gladly, and turned to smile at his keeper, who was waiting by his side with a fresh gun.

'Well done, sir,' said Tom. He handed over the loaded gun, and began emptying the cartridges out of the first to reload.

Harris said, 'Great Christ, look at that!'

An enormous red-brown bird was swooping down out of the sky. Tom looked up just in time to see it pause, hold the air in its wings … and then suddenly snatch Harris's shot bird right out of the air. It sank slightly in the wind from the weight of the pheasant, swung its feet back, and began to fly rapidly away towards the woods with the bird held firmly in its claws.

'It's a bloody poacher, Mase!' laughed Harris. 'That's a sight you don't see every day!'

Harris barked, 'Mine!' in case anyone else wanted a go at the bird. His gun jumped to his shoulder but the kite was already almost out of range. It got close to the woods when it heard the beaters crashing about inside. It wheeled round, paused in the sky for a second as it checked the lie of the land, then flew in a straight line directly at Harris.

'Dead bird, Mase,' grinned Harris. He took aim but the bird was a fast flyer ... and ... BANG! Taylor and Alan couldn't run straight out of the woods in case they got their heads blown off. They had to run to one side and come out behind the guns. They got there just in time to see Teresa stalling in the air as the pellets blasted into her.

Taylor screamed, 'No!' One or two of the guns turned to look at him. Teresa dropped the pheasant and dived in a great curve, like a plane falling out of the sky. For a second she seemed to recover in the air and began to half fly, half glide into the woods.

There was a second shot from somewhere. Teresa flinched in the air before she crashed into the trees at the edge of the woodland.

Harris cursed. He turned to Tom. 'Get some of the men to sort the thing out, Mase.'

'Will do, sir,' said Tom. As he spoke Taylor and Alan came running up. Both men turned to them.

'It's a protected bird, sir, you can't shoot it,' said Taylor, panting.

Harris stared not at the boy, but at Tom.

'Boy's bird mad, sir,' said Tom quietly.

Harris grinned. 'Vermin everywhere, Mase,' he laughed.

Tom flushed as he realised what the man meant. Harris was furious. Being criticised by the keeper's snotty little son!

They were interrupted. A tall man with a red beard, one of the guns, pushed his way forward from amongst the other guns.

'The boy's right. That was a red kite. Are you aware how many of those there are left?'

'One less, now, I should hope,' said Harris insolently.

The man looked at him in disgust. 'People like you...' he began.

But Harris turned sharply to Tom. 'See this gentleman off my land, will you, Mase?' he said loudly. His face had turned purple.

The tall man snorted. 'You're not fit to own a back garden. I'll see this gets dealt with.'

Tom touched him gently on his elbow and pointed the way to one of the Land Rovers.

'Bloody vermin gets everywhere,' said Harris in a loud voice to the other guests.

Some of them laughed uneasily, but many were looking worried, even angry, as the news of what had happened spread around. The shooters were not all like Harris. Many of them loved watching the wildlife as much as they did shooting at it.

There was a pause of some fifteen minutes while the beaters searched for the wounded bird. Dogs were sent in, but she couldn't be found.

Harris couldn't wait. His guests had paid good money to shoot pheasants. He ordered the beaters on to the next patch. Taylor and Alan wanted to stay behind to search on, but Taylor's dad wouldn't hear of it. He took the chance to give Taylor a rare cuff round the ear.

'You stay out of his way … and mine. Do you want to get us all into trouble?' he barked.

There were two more drives before the day was over. Alan and Taylor were counting the seconds to the time when they could go and hunt for Teresa but to their disgust they were sent straight home, made to go back even though their Teresa was bleeding and maybe dying in the woods.

Taylor couldn't believe it. His dad was everything to him. Didn't he understand how precious this bird was? Alan stood watching while Taylor begged and pleaded, but Tom was tired, stressed, and furious with Taylor for arguing with him. On the way home Taylor wept with hatred and fury.

'I'll never forgive him for this,' he cried bitterly. 'I'll never forgive him.'

Alan watched his hero's tears with a white face. And the Great Tom Mase, father of Taylor, was behaving like a Harris! He would have cried for Teresa himself, but the sight of Taylor seemed to freeze the tears in his throat.

Suddenly he had a thought. 'Maybe we should tell Teddy.'

He was sorry as soon as he'd said it. You didn't fight Harris.

But Taylor stared at him fiercely. 'Yes! We can write to him. Tell him.'

'But what about your dad? What about your house?'

'Sod my dad! We'll both write, so he knows it's true. Tonight!'

'What about you robbing the nest?'

'I don't care. Well, we won't tell him that, of course. We'll write our letters when we get home, and we'll show them to each other tomorrow at school before we post them. Okay?'

'Okay.'

They looked at each other's faces. Then Taylor swung away and ran back home.

It had been a good day for Tom; the bag was over six hundred birds. In the backs of the Land Rovers were heaped mountains of bodies. Tom went round to each gun to deliver a complimentary brace of pheasants and to collect a tip. The rest of the birds would be off to market in the morning. Then he paid off the beaters, complimented Old John on their day's work and shared out the money.

Only then, in darkness, his gun under his arm and his dog at his heel, did he make his way back home.

The estate was silent. The woodland, which had been so lovingly cared for all year long, was stunned by the massacre. The little birds trembled in the twigs. Even the mice were scared to rustle among the fallen leaves and dry grasses by the roadside.

As for the pheasants, they had disappeared deep into the woods. It would be days before they would be seen again strutting in the open fields.

What a slaughter, thought Tom. Their Little Darlings ...
betrayed! His own favourite, the white pheasant Dan the
Man, hung with the others by his feet, dripping blood
from his beak onto the floor of the game larder. He would
not pass on his beautiful feathers after all.

Tom paused at the edge of his garden to look back into
the woods. It was so still, as if even the trees were in shock.

'Bloody slaughter,' he said aloud. Then he pushed open
the gate and went in to feed the dogs before bed.

Eleven

Harris's shot had not killed Teresa outright.

The blast of shot and the terrible pain, in her breast and wing almost stunned her. She had only just managed to stay in the air long enough to crash into a tall ash tree, and clung onto a branch close to the trunk. Her left wing hung by her side in a blaze of agony, broken in two places by the shot. Here she stayed while the men searched for her on the ground and then left.

She had survived, but there was an end to the catching of the wind. Few birds survive a broken wing and ever fly again, unless the break is close to the wing tip. Teresa's was broken close to her body. It would never hold her weight again.

It was in the same place, huddled up to the trunk of the ash tree some forty feet above the ground, that the jackdaws found her. They had been feeding amongst the manure spread on the fields nearby when they had been disturbed by the sound of gunfire. They flew in a panic and hid in the trees around the wounded kite, They were shocked at first, sharing a tree with such a big predator. But they were five, she was only one. They mobbed her, and when they realised that she was injured, they were delighted.

Teresa hunched her shoulders and ducked her head as the birds dive-bombed her. The jackdaws grew bold and began to beat at her with their wings and strike at her with their sharp stout beaks and soon the inevitable happened.

She lost her footing and fell, a fluttering, bewildered ball of agony, to land with a crash forty feet below.

She lay there unconscious while the jackdaws flew down to peck her eyes out. But now the guns saved her. The shooting started up again a few hundred yards away and the frightened daws tore off in a panic, leaving their fun and the chance of a fat meal. They forgot Teresa and went to wait in the church tower, where they stayed until the shooting was over.

Had Tom let him stay and search, Taylor would have found her lying on her back under the ash tree. But he was a quarter of a mile away, weeping with rage and frustration.

The wounded bird recovered enough to crawl into a patch of dense thorns. The close branches and sharp jags caught at her wing but at least they offered some sort of protection. There she stayed until nightfall, when she tried to climb higher into the thorns to roost, but soon gave up the painful effort. She settled to sleep on the ground, and relied on the thorns to keep her enemies at bay.

At about the same time that Tom was making his way home, another woodland dweller was making her way across the meadows east of the woods.

As she paused on the gravelly edge of a stream crossing the meadow, a young vixen sniffed at the air and tasted the heavy, rich smell of spilled blood.

The vixen could smell other things as well: warm skin, tobacco, hot metal, oil and, above all, gunshot and powder. The vixen was only a year old, quick as a weasel and as clever as any beast in the land, but she lacked the experience to know what those other smells might mean. She had grown up in a railway cutting and since leaving home she had stayed in the cutting, travelling west, feeding on voles and young rabbits. She knew enough to keep away from trains, but about man she knew next to nothing.

The blood on the air tasted good. Not all of it was old. There were wounded birds in the woods. Some were not far away. There were no other foxes.

All this her nose told her. The vixen slipped across the fields and paused at the wire bordering the trees. She tasted the air once again. She could hardly believe her good luck. She slipped under the wire, took a dozen steps among the trees, tested the air one more time and then trotted off to find her dinner.

Within twenty feet she passed right over the spot where Teresa had fallen from the ash tree, and stopped on a penny. She sniffed the ground. Four steps took her to the clump of thorns. She snuffed at the air under the thorn bushes. It was a bird, a falcon. It was bleeding and sick. It was on the ground. It was scared silly.

The vixen pressed her white belly flat against the leaf litter and slid in after her.

Teresa was awake from the moment the fox stopped to sniff at her trail. She knew the scent of fox. A creature of the day, her eyes were crippled in the night: a creature of the air, her wings were crippled with lead shot. Although she was almost blind in the woodland night, she turned her great bright eyes to face her enemy and prepared to die.

She stayed still as long as she dared. Maybe, just maybe, the fox would pass her by. She waited bravely until the vixen actually began to nose her way into the thorns only five feet away, before she lowered her head and tried to run for it. There was a sudden electric thrill as the vixen heard her. She froze in her tracks. Her sharp ears twitched; she knew to the inch where the sounds were coming from. She spun to the right and bounded forward to make her kill – and pricked her nose horribly on the little daggers of blackthorn.

The vixen yelped and paused to lick her nose. Then she growled dangerously. The taste of her own blood made her cross – and hungrier than ever. She stooped low to sniff the air under the twigs. Her nose might be pricked, but it was as sharp as ever. It told her exactly where the kite was – sitting in a deep cluster of thorns less than a yard away. But … infuriating! An impenetrable barrier of thorns was in the way. The vixen, still growling loudly, began to circle round to try and find a way in.

Teresa was listening for her life. In the darkness within the bushes, she turned her head round like an owl as she followed the fox's progress around her.

Now a deadly game of hide-and-seek began. Every time the fox got near, clever Teresa darted off through the close little branches. And every single time the silly vixen got over-excited and jumped at her and got a nose full of thorns. Pretty soon she was viciously, spitefully cross, growling and yelping and yapping to try and scare Teresa out. But it was no game to Teresa. Her broken wing was savaged by the thorns, she was weak, the thorn bush was small …

It was surely only a matter of time.

Then at last Teresa made a mistake. She pushed through the thorns as the fox got close, and fell onto the leaf litter outside the thicket. The fox yelped in excitement, did a double turn on a penny, doubled back and jumped through a narrow gap in the thorns. Teresa picked herself up and there was the fox, her carrion-stinking breath right in her face, half in, half out of the thorns, struggling like a maniac to escape and finish it off. Without thinking, Teresa tried her usual means of escape – the air. She bounded up and flapped her wings, screaming in pain, and just managed to grab at a bough of low-hanging field maple. The bough swung low; Teresa hung a foot from the ground like a fruit ready to pick. The fox jumped out and up – and her mouth closed tight on the kite's tail feathers.

By the time she shook her head free of the tickles, Teresa had climbed out of reach.

The vixen was furious. Her nose had been pricked so often it felt as big as an apple. The bird was wounded and weak and perfectly ready to eat – and now suddenly it was out of reach.

She sat a while to consider her tactics. Above her she could hear the kite clawing her way higher into the bushes, but in this light she could not see her. She tried an experimental leap up into the dark, but all she got was her face lashed with twigs and small branches.

She sat down again, licking her lips. Then she snorted with disgust, got up, and walked away. Teresa, safe in a tree at last, listened to the soft footfalls on the fallen leaves. If she'd had tears, now she would have shed them. Instead, she began to shiver violently. It felt as if her whole body was about to fall apart. She crouched low on her branch, locked her feet, closed her eyes and tried to sleep.

Meanwhile, the vixen of course had not given up at all. Going away was simply another trick in her pack. She made what for her was a great deal of noise going away up-wind, and then circled about and came back down-wind in utter silence. There she sat, hidden under an elder bush with a few ragged yellow leaves still left on its branches, and listened for signs of movement from the kite. But Teresa had no reason to move and stayed put.

The vixen was so furious with Teresa that she would gladly have waited all night and all day – as long it took to get that bird between her jaws. But she had to eat, so after about an hour she stood up, shook herself, and went off to find other prey.

It was not the end of the matter as far as she was concerned. She had no intention of leaving these fine woods, so full of prey, so heavy with blood. She knew Teresa would not be flying off. Later that night she'd call again – and the next night, and the night after, and the night after that. As long as it took. Now that she had lost the sky there was nowhere Teresa could go, but the fox could follow. Sooner or later, she'd get her chance.

Next morning Taylor was up at first light to get in some hours of searching before school. But, Tom was already waiting there to tell him he was grounded for a week. He was outraged at his son's stupidity – telling Harris off! Taylor had made him look a fool.

Taylor could hardly talk, he was so full of outrage. It was Harris who was in the wrong, his father knew that! He was barely able to argue through his tears. As soon as Tom left for work, Taylor ran out of the house himself and made his way to the patch of woodland where Teresa had been shot. Behind him his mother yelled furiously.

'Your dad'll skin you alive!'

But Taylor took no notice. Let his father rage. What did he care for him?

That morning he scoured the patch of woodland leaf by leaf. He had his binoculars with him and he examined every tree, every branch. At one point he thought he heard her call, but when he went to the place and called back to her, 'Puss, puss, puss!' There was no answer. Afterwards he paid a visit to the gibbet and looked behind the rhododendron bushes for freshly dug earth. He found the grave of the kite his father had killed. The newest grave was only a week or so old. He had helped dig it himself to house a young mongrel pup belonging to a new family in the village, which had taken to chasing the pheasants. But nothing had been dug in the last couple of days.

Taylor stood in the wet grass and touched his inside pocket, where a piece of paper rustled crisply, the letter to Teddy Harris.

Telling on the bully. Going behind his back. And Harris was such a bully that he could turn you out of your home if he felt like it. Taylor rubbed his face. The stakes were so high! But he hated his father now.

As he ran round the hut to check the gibbet itself, he didn't see a figure standing in the damp leafy cover just off the clearing. Tom hushed his dog and made it lie down as he watched his son search and weep.

Tom was furious, but he was also impressed. Taylor could be a villain with some folk but he never usually disobeyed his father. He didn't interrupt, but waited quietly until Taylor was gone. He had some idea of why his son was so desperate about the kite. He knew all about the 'buzzard' in Alan's garage. In a village the size of Hale secrets didn't keep long. And, of course, someone had stolen the kite's eggs from the nest that spring. He had heard the boys call this bird Teresa. How did she come to get a name so quickly?

Well, the boy was devoted all right. And it took some courage to tick Harris off like that. That was worth something.

Tom wondered if maybe he ought to be proud of his son rather than punish him.

Teresa roosted that first night in the field maple, and saw the dawn come up in pain, and burning with thirst.

For a long time she waited in the tree. She knew how dangerous the woodland floor was. A cold, damp wind blew, stirring the few blackened leaves left on the trees. As the mists were lifting, she heard Taylor crashing through the forest calling her. 'Teresa! Teresa! Here, puss, puss, puss!' And had he passed under that tree and looked up he might have seen her, the big red bird crookedly perched only ten feet or so off the ground. But Taylor was blinded with anger and in a hurry. He had school waiting for him. Although he passed nearby he did not see her.

As he walked further into the distance, memories of fat jays overcame her and she called out to him once. Taylor heard and doubled back excitedly. In the woods it was difficult to trace the call. He came close, but Teresa was scared as he came near. She was in no mood to trust anyone. She lowered her head and kept quiet.

The morning wore on. The thirst was burning her throat. Teresa tried to nibble moisture from the dying leaves.

At about ten o'clock a little breeze sprang up from deeper within the woods and stirred the kite's feathers and the twigs of the maple. On this breeze was carried a most delicious and appetising scent. Teresa blinked and lifted up her head. She opened her mouth as if the scent could fill her belly. If she'd had any lips she would have smacked them. Mmmm ... yes!

It was the thick stink of rotting flesh. Liver and muscle and eyes and guts, buzzing with flies. Delicious!

Holding her head up, her mouth open to take in the delightful scent, Teresa hopped along her branch and tried to flutter onto the next tree. Disaster! She fell and landed with a hard thud on the dead damp leaves. She got to her feet at once, panting with pain. One good thing came of it, though. When she hit the ground a small white slug was flung out of cover. Teresa found it and pecked it up. Lovely – moist, cool and soothing.

Fortified by her slug, she began to hop and run in short little dashes towards the enticing smell. Her broken wing trailed behind her, dragging painfully over the twigs and roots. She had to push her way through bushes and skip over fallen branches. But that smell! It was worth every twinge. By now the pain of her wounds was less than the gnawing hunger in her belly, and the need to slake her thirst on cold, damp, rotting meat. It had been days since she had eaten a decent meal.

The gorgeous smell was coming from the bottom of a steep slope. Almost running now, ducking under trees and bushes, slipping on the crumbly earth, Teresa at last came within sight of her dinner table ...

The gibbet. There, lined up in neat rows along the wooden walls, was a kite's feast waiting to be eaten.

Teresa ran up to the foot of the wooden wall. Jays, just like the ones Taylor and Alan had fed her! She jumped up to try and get her talons into them but that wing was agony. Every movement jarred the broken edges of bone. But she had to eat. Jumping, falling back, trying again, the kite at last managed to get her talons into one of the dead birds. There she hung for ten seconds or so, half upside down like an enormous moth at a strange flower. She glanced once, twice over her shoulder to see if all was still, before she pecked into the ripe flesh.

Some time later, when her hunger was satisfied, Teresa dropped back down to the ground and made her way back into cover. On the edges of the clearing she found an ancient rhododendron tree sweeping close to the ground. Using the branches like a ladder, she was able to climb up high and out of sight.

And here she stayed.

Where better? Why move on? Her wounds were crippling, but not fatal. Given enough to eat she could live for years, and here was a supply of food a scavenger like a kite would die for.

Yet there were many enemies. Tom and Harris, to name two of them. There was the half-eaten body of a jay on the gibbet, waiting to be spotted. Tom would know vermin was feeding on the gibbet flesh before the day was out. And the vixen had not forgotten her prey. That very night she found Teresa's scent on the ground and followed her to the rhododendron. She even went so far as to climb up on the big lower branches to get a good look.

The fox sat below on a black branch and growled in her throat, loud enough to let Teresa know she had not forgotten. That night she too made her meal from the larder that Tom and John had so thoughtfully provided.

The vixen would be back. She would always approach

the gibbet downwind, so that Teresa would smell and hear nothing of her until she arrived. One day, perhaps, she would catch Teresa hanging ready to be plucked from a jay or a magpie, and it would all be over.

But the world did not hold only enemies. Taylor and Alan had not yet given up hope of finding her alive.

Twelve

At the time when Teresa was hopping and crawling her way over the woodland floor towards the gibbet, Taylor and Alan were sitting in their classrooms chewing their nails and gazing out of the window. The minutes and hours crawled by. At breaktime Taylor usually played football with his classmates. He felt Alan was too young for him at school. But this time they got together to compare their letters.

'Dear Mr Harris...'

They always called him Teddy to each other. It seemed funny complaining to Mr Harris about Mr Harris, but they got there in the end. Alan had pinched a couple of envelopes from his mum. They tucked the letters inside, licked them down and wrote the address on the front.

'We can get some stamps after school,' said Taylor.

'Are we really going to send them?' Alan wanted to know.

Taylor was sure. 'Definitely,' he replied. He thought of his father grounding him this week of all weeks, just when Teresa needed him. 'Definitely,' he said.

At last the school day drew to a close. They ran to the village post office, bought their stamps and posted their letters. It was awful letting go of them and watching them drop down into the stomach of the post box. It was done now, there was no going back. Telling on the bully. What would happen now?

Then they ran straight to the place where Taylor had heard Teresa call that morning.

'Are you sure you heard her?'

'I'm sure. I know her!' said Taylor, although he wasn't at all sure.

They ran through the patch of woods where she had been shot, crawled under the hedges and even poked into the thorn thicket. There was a moment of great excitement when Alan found a couple of her tail feathers under the field maple.

They almost tore the thorn bushes to bits with long sticks to get to the inside. But Teresa had left hours before while they still sat at their desks, and they found nothing.

They ran on through the woods, calling and searching, crawling and yelling out Teresa's feeding call, 'Puss, puss, puss!' They came to the gibbet several times and even peered into the rhododendron. Up high, hidden among the thick green leaves, Teresa hunkered down and gripped hard with her claws. The boys had no idea that they were just yards away from her. They left without seeing the torn jay, still hanging on the wall, that had been her breakfast.

Taylor went home that evening with a black heart, expecting fury from his father for disobeying his orders. But Tom was not so hard. No more was said about the grounding. When he came into the living room that evening, Tom turned down the radio and asked him, 'Any luck?'

Taylor shook his head.

'You might as well face it, Taylor, the bird's dead. You know how long a wounded hawk lasts on the ground.'

Taylor looked away to hide his face.

'I'm sorry about it. You know what I think of Harris, but I have to work.'

'There are other jobs,' said Taylor, repeating what he'd heard Teddy Harris say once.

Tom tapped his thumbs together irritably.

'Anyway, I heard her calling,' said Taylor. 'I heard her. She might still be alive.'

Tom pulled a face. 'There was a buzzard circling over Lord's Wood this morning.'

'It was her,' insisted Taylor.

Tom shook his head. 'Even if it was ... a bird like that has just too many enemies, Taylor. You know that. Harris is seething. I reckon he'd pay you in gold to have that bird chopped up and fed to the pigs. Pricey bacon that would be,' he added, and he gave his son a little smile, willing him to make friends.

Taylor scowled. He would have liked to make friends. He understood what his father was saying, but surely he could have been allowed to search for Teresa after the shoot?

'No shortage of pigs around here,' he said insolently.

Tom's head jerked up angrily. Taylor, turned his back quickly and ran up to his room, but Tom was behind him and caught him a mighty whack on the bum as he jumped up the stairs.

'You keep a civil tongue in your head,' he yelled.

'I'm sorry, all right? Thanks.'

Tom paused. 'All right, then. Go on, get to bed.'

119

The following day when he returned home from school there was an owl hooting in the sitting room. Teddy Harris had arrived.

The old man looked just the same – fluffy hair and floppy ears. He was dressed in a green tweed suit. He stared at Taylor with enormous pale blue eyes. 'Shot it? He *shot* it?' he demanded as Taylor told his story.

'Bang, right out of the sky.' Taylor watched Teddy's eyes fill with water and overflow. He thought about adding that his dad had handed Harris the gun, but thought better of it.

All the blood drained out of Teddy's face until he looked like a pale shell. Then his ears began to burn red with rage. Reg had sworn blind he would help protect the kites! He might have known. He'd been a sneak and a liar as a child, and age had only made him worse. Teddy was so furious he started pulling hairs out of his beard. 'I'll bloody kill him!' he snarled. He twisted on his heel and dashed to the door.

Taylor's mother was waiting anxiously in the hall.

'But you won't tell him Taylor told you, will you, Mr Harris? It's a shame about the birds, I know. But…'

Teddy was hopping about from one foot to the other and trembling with his desire to get his hands on Harris. He grunted – it could have meant anything – and ran out. Seconds later they heard his old Morris car coughing and wheezing in the driveway, before he sped off with a squeal and a scattering of gravel.

Anne turned furiously on Taylor.

'You stupid, stupid child!'

Taylor was shocked, but he stuck to his guns. 'He killed a kite, it's illegal ...' he began.

'Do you think your dad likes working for Harris? Do you think he wouldn't take another job if he could find one? Well, I'll tell you this. If Harris finds out who told on him, we'll be out of a house and out of work. And if we find ourselves living in some horrid little town with nothing but grey streets for miles around and no money, you'll know whose fault it is. And this is the boy who keeps asking me to buy a television! Wait till your father finds out about this!'

Taylor went up to his bedroom feeling sick. He was dying to have a television. Alan's family had one, a great hot thing that showed fascinating fuzzy grey pictures. He'd watched cartoons and pop programmes on it.

Well, he'd let go of the television if he had to. But his house, too? Did it really have to cost so much?

Taylor was surprised and shocked at how upset his mum was, and his dad, when he came home. It was easy for him – he didn't have to worry about money. It was easy for Teddy Harris, too, who didn't have to do a stroke of work unless the fancy took him. Tom and Anne both knew what it was to be out of work with no money. They had a life in Hale Magna and they didn't want to lose it. But it was humiliating to have to depend on the goodwill of a man like Harris.

Teddy found Harris standing outside the house drinking a cup of tea. He braked to a violent skid and jumped out.

'You're a bastard, Reg!'

'Uncle! What?'

Teddy let out a volley of abuse. Liar … hypocrite … bully … thug… vandal … Harris listened and started to bulge. Behind him, Mrs Dell, his housekeeper, came out to wash the steps and make sure she got every word to repeat to the other servants. Harris turned round to glare at her.

'I'll not have you speak like that to me in front of the servants!' he yelped.

'You were a selfish, spoiled brat of a child, and now you're a selfish, spoiled brat of man!' shrilled Teddy. 'I told you … the bloody things eat CARRION!'

Harris bared his teeth. He could have broken Teddy between his hands but … Uncle Teddy was a rich man. Harris was expecting some inheritance from him when he died.

He spread his hands. 'I *saw* it, Ted! It lifted one of my birds right out of …'

'I don't care what it did. You'd do better banning cars; they kill more birds every month than a couple of kites do in a year – you ignorant, spoiled, lying toad!'

'That's a bit strong!'

'Idiot!'

There was a snort of agreement behind them. Harris turned round to glare. Mrs Dell squeezed out her cloth into the bucket and nodded vigorously.

'Can't we discuss this inside?' he pleaded.

'No we can't!'

'I didn't even know what it was … I thought it was a peregrine …' lied Reg.

'I've a mind to leave your inheritance to the kite trust in Wales. You're a bastard, Reg, a lying little bastard!'

Harris swelled up with rage. 'Uncle … please …' he begged. He was grinding the road under his feet in rage and frustration. The whole house was listening but he didn't dare yell back. Harris wasn't as rich as he made out. He was counting on that money in the next ten or twenty years.

Even so, he was wondering if it was worth any amount of money by the time Teddy had finished with him. He spent fifteen minutes screaming at him in full hearing of the whole house, and then made him give instructions to Tom and John to leave the birds of prey alone whenever they saw them.

To make matters worse, the old man insisted on staying on to search the woods for the missing bird, and of course he had to get Taylor and Alan involved. The final humiliation for Harris was when he came back to the house one evening to find Teddy taking tea with Taylor and Alan in the sitting room.

The two boys sprang to their feet as he came into the room. Harris jumped and yelped, he was so surprised.

'Ah, Reg, just in time for a cup and a slice of Mrs Dell's fruit cake …' said Teddy, rattling the lid of the teapot. 'Sit down, boys,' he added.

Taylor and Alan sank back quivering onto the twelve-foot-long sofa. They felt like two rabbits taking tea in the fox's den. As for Harris, he was unable to utter a word. He smiled like a man who'd just had an accident in his pants and walked back out.

'When are you just going to go and die?' he hissed at the door. He ran upstairs and drank a large whisky, and refused to come down until the two boys had left.

Harris grinned like a dog when he met Tom on the driveway the next morning. 'Glad to see your son's being so cooperative with my uncle, Mase,' he said pleasantly.

Tom got straight to the point. 'I know it must be galling, sir, but the fact is I have no reason to stop him. What would I say to your uncle? I can't tell him that you don't like it, now, can I?'

Harris scowled and drew close. 'When the old fool goes,' he said, 'the only thing in feathers I want to see round here is pheasants. Understand, Mase?'

'I understand, sir.'

'Trust me to have mad relatives.' Harris truly believed that he was the only normal person in the world. Now he had bird cranks crawling all over his land and his gamekeeper's son was helping them! All because of one bloody bird.

Teddy, Taylor and Alan turned the woods over leaf by leaf. The old man's eyes weren't as sharp as they once had been, but he could still pick up the slightest flicker of a feather where the boys stared and stared and saw nothing but leaves.

They saw any number of birds: nuthatch, tree-creeper,

bullfinch, three kinds of woodpecker, goldcrests, wrens and the long-eared owls that had survived in the pine plantation, to name just a few. But of Teresa they saw nothing. There was evidence, but expert as Teddy was, he did not have the knowledge to recognise the damage on the gibbet as the work of a kite. He saw the half-eaten bodies and put it down to crows and paid it no notice.

At the end of a week, by way of saying thanks, he took Taylor and Alan on a day trip to Dartmoor, birdwatching. They took sandwiches and marched around the tors armed with Teddy's binoculars and a borrowed pair of Harris's, to Harris's unspeakable disgust. They saw buzzards – ten in the sky at once at one point. They saw grouse and ring ouzels and a great shaggy raven. 'The vulture of the moor,' Teddy called it. They marked off each species on their sheets, and added up how many types of bird they had seen so far that year.

The high spot of the day, though, was the sight of a rare Montagu's harrier circling among the buzzards around a high tor. The flight was light and quick compared to the heavy buzzards.

'Just like Teresa!' exclaimed Alan.

Taylor kicked him in the leg. He and Alan were only supposed to have seen the kite just as Harris shot it, hardly enough to be clear how it flew.

Teddy pursed his lips and asked no questions. But a little later he stared at them with his big blue eyes and said, 'You'll look after the birds from now on, won't you, boys?'

'We promise, don't we, Alan?' insisted Taylor.

Alan looked sulky. He wanted to tell the old man how Taylor had rescued the egg and they'd brought the bird up. But only Taylor knew that wasn't the whole story. Anyway, what difference did it make? It was too late. If the kite had been alive, Teddy would have been bound to find some sort of clue or other. Harris had been given a good scolding, but he'd got it his way after all. Teresa was certainly dead.

Thirteen

Up in her leafy roost, Teresa quietly watched the various visitors to the gibbet come and go, and stayed as still and as quiet as if she really were dead. She saw Teddy and the two boys creeping around. Later Taylor came with his dad, helping him nail weasels by their snouts and hanging jays and crows by their feet. Whenever he came to the gibbet he would glance sideways at the place where the owls and hawks hung, just in case ...

It seemed only natural to Teresa that Taylor should fetch food for her. He did it when she was a chick; he was still doing it now. That was what Taylor was for. Whenever she saw him coming she always clucked to herself and fluffed her feathers affectionately. But she never called to him. She had other memories of Taylor too: Taylor shouting and banging and dragging her around on a piece of string. Taylor calling her down from the sky into the blaze of gunshot.

With food at her disposal, Teresa's wounds began to mend quickly. Her wing was still too sore to try to use, but within a couple of weeks she was feeling well enough to start watching with interest the family of rats who crawled up the walls from the inside to feast on the carrion. One morning at dawn when she came out to feed, she crept quietly as a cat across the long grass of the clearing and hid beneath the gibbet, waiting for a brown, quivering snout to appear. Sure enough, there it was, poking through a hole in the rotten wooden walls. The rat eyed Teresa suspiciously, but it had seen her often enough to think her harmless. It crawled out of the wall, and began to sniff hungrily at a green-shrouded weasel.

Teresa leapt up with a flutter of wings and a little cry – it hurt! – and snatched with her beak. But she was far too slow. The rat squealed in surprise and jumped back into the shed.

Every day Teresa tried her luck. The rats learned to stay out of reach. They waddled about in between the corpses and gnawed old meat from the tops of the walls while Teresa ran this way and that in the grass in excitement. Day by day her strength increased, and the rats had to climb higher and higher. Then came the day she actually caught one. The rats had grown lazy. She knocked a fat old grandmother off the wall, fell to earth right on top of it and struck a single, skull-crushing blow to its head. Above her, the wall cleared of rats. Teresa peered around her, lowered her head, and began to feed.

Soon after the rats stopped coming out at dawn and stuck to the night time for feeding. But there were enemies in the dark, too. The tawny owl who lived in an old elm nearby soon learned the same trick. He took to waiting close by at night and listening for the scurry and squeaks of the rats coming out to feed.

The owl was even worse than the kite. At least they could see her running along in the grass under the gibbet, whereas the first warning they had of him was the thud and squeak of a death. So the rats went back to feeding during the day, and Teresa got her sport back. It was a dangerous game, though. Every few months or so Tom or John put down poison to clear the rats out of the shed. If Teresa ate any of the sudden windfall of corpses then, she would die.

Her wounds were healing. Her wing no longer hurt so badly and she was soon tempted to try it on the wind. She stood high in an open space inside her tree and lifted her wings. But the hollow bones of birds never knit together well once they've been broken. The ends of the broken bone stayed apart; the wing wagged like a torn branch on a tree and hurt her badly. Teresa had to learn to live life more like a squirrel than a bird. Her world had shrunk from countrywide to the width of a single tree.

Meanwhile the visitors came and went. Most nights the vixen called by. She was too clever and too fond of hunting to steal from the gibbet every night, but every now and then she helped herself to a nice, fresh crow. She always made a point of climbing a few yards up the rhododendron tree and growling at Teresa to make her shuffle and flap in the dark, in the hope that she might fall down.

Harris was another visitor. Teresa got to know that tuneless whistle as he pushed his way down the slope and counted the new arrivals on the shed wall. And of course she saw Tom almost every day.

The gamekeeper knew that the gibbet attracted vermin. Crows and magpies loved carrion, foxes were not above taking dead meat. Each day when he came to the gibbet he approached quietly, downwind, so as to get a shot at anything that might be feeding there. Teresa saw everything. She watched him as he peered at the little dead bodies she had torn as she fed and bent to touch the marks the vixen's feet made beneath the gibbet wall.

That week Tom came twice before dawn and hid in the bushes, waiting for the fox to come by. But the vixen was careful, too. She always circled the place several times before going in. She smelt him in hiding and stayed away from the gibbet that night. Tom stayed like a stump of wood watching the dew gather on his clothes until the daylight opened up the woods, before he stretched and cursed his wasted night.

Had he waited a little longer Tom would certainly have caught Teresa running out of the bushes for her feed. He had known for some time that a large bird was feeding almost daily, and he guessed it might very well be the kite. The bird had been shot near here, after all. Just on the off-chance he spent a half hour peering up into the trees, but he saw nothing.

From then on, whenever he came to the gibbet Tom came more quietly than ever, peering through the leaves with his gun at the ready. He said nothing to Taylor about it, though. Why make more trouble for himself? Harris was bad enough to work for as it was without Taylor playing him up.

A few weeks after the shooting, Harris had yet another nasty surprise when the local policeman, PC Vanes, knocked on the door to arrest him under the Protection of Birds Act. Harris, who thought of the police as the people who helped keep the poachers down, couldn't believe that such laws existed, or if they did that anyone would have the nerve to do this to him.

'Don't be so bloody stupid,' he yelled, and slammed the door in the poor man's face. Then he stormed indoors to write a letter of complaint to the Chief Constable.

The reply came back to the effect that Vanes was only doing his duty, but Harris didn't really believe anything would come of it. It still seemed like something that was happening to someone else when, a few weeks before Christmas, he was summoned to appear before the local magistrate.

Harris was found guilty and fined thirty pounds. Half of the people present on the shoot that day had been prepared to turn up and give evidence, so there was no shortage of witnesses. The magistrate, a pompous little headmaster from a nearby grammar school, was scathing towards Harris, whom he called 'a throwback to the dark ages'. The fine of thirty pounds wasn't much to Harris, but being told off publicly infuriated him. Even worse than that, though, was the coverage in the press.

The local paper ran it on the front page: 'THE SHAME OF THE WEST COUNTRY!' with a big photo of Harris frothing outside the court. It was a good shot. There were his rolling eyes and his scruffy beard and you got a good look halfway up his nose, which made him look ridiculous. Then the national papers got hold of it and used the same picture with the headline: 'THE BEAST OF HALE MAGNA.'

Taylor cut the article out and posted it to Teddy, who rang his nephew up and gave him another scolding for bringing the family into disrepute. Harris was not a popular man locally, either. Several village people put the picture up in their windows and it made him tremble with rage every time he saw it. Although it was obviously the tall man with the red beard who had complained on the day of the shoot who had shopped him, Harris tried to blame anyone he could lay his hands on for it. He gave Taylor a really hard cuff round the ear one day, just in case he had had anything to do with it. He even tried to blame Mrs Dell, who refused to come round and do for him for a week until he sent her a note apologising for his bad behaviour.

He suspected Tom as well as everyone else, and the two men had a furious row in the woods one day when Harris suggested it was him. Tom was livid with the unjust accusation and told him he could stuff his job if he wasn't prepared to trust him. Harris backed off; he knew he had a good man in Tom Mase. But Tom was getting to the point where he was ready to pack it in on his own account.

Taylor thought a lot better of his dad when he heard the story. In his mind the kite was dead, it was all over, and he loved Tom too much to be able to stay so angry with him. It helped that he was standing up to Harris. He might have thought differently had he known that Tom suspected that Teresa was still alive, and was creeping around the gibbet clearing once or twice a week in the hope of getting a shot at her.

Meanwhile, Harris stormed around in a fury and swore to destroy anything bigger than a blue tit that dared enter his woods.

Fourteen

Christmas came, and the weather was soft and damp. Pale mists hung between the trees. On Christmas Eve Taylor's mum and dad had some friends round and played records until past midnight. Taylor lay in bed and listened to the strains of Elvis and Buddy Holly float upstairs. He was still awake when he heard footsteps crunch on the gravel outside, and the voices calling goodbye.

A little later his mum and dad staggered up the stairs to put his presents at the foot of his bed. Taylor had stopped believing in Father Christmas years before, but they carried on the game anyway. It was still exciting to wake up to presents heaped like magic at the foot of the bed.

Tom and Anne had drunk too much and kept dropping things and falling against the walls, and going, 'Sssh … sssh!' Taylor pretended to be asleep, and waited until it was all done and they were almost out of the room before he sat up and said, 'Father Christmas is a bit drunk this year, isn't he?'

'You swine, Taylor, I thought you were asleep!'

Taylor sat up in bed and laughed at them. His mum and dad came in to give their son boozy kisses, and he fell straight to sleep.

In the morning, he gently patted the neatly wrapped presents on his bed, but something made him get up to look out of the window first. There, in the still mist, were three deer eating the winter cabbages.

Taylor was entranced. Deer in the garden on Christmas morning; it was like a blessing. He let the curtain quietly fall and went to fetch his mum and dad so they could see it, too.

'Jesus, it's only seven o'clock, Taylor!' groaned his mother. But Taylor was certain they had to see it. He pushed, teased and cajoled them out of bed and down the passage to his room, but when they peered out of the curtains the deer were gone.

'Jesus wept,' groaned his mother, and lurched off back to bed.

'But they were there. Look, you can see their footprints in the grass,' pointed out Taylor.

His dad winked. 'I told you you can sometimes see God's footprints on the lawn,' he said, and went back to bed. Taylor frowned at the barely remembered phrase from years ago. But it seemed somehow to him that his dad was right.

He got a new bike from his mum and dad, and a pair of binoculars from Teddy Harris. 'May you see a kite through them one day!' he wrote on his card, and Taylor felt a pang right through his stomach.

The weather stayed mild for weeks; it was as if autumn was going to go on all winter. In January it was wet and windy, but in early February, at last, came the real cold. The month turned with the woods sparkling under hoar frosts, layer after layer of crystals growing on twigs like tiny, hard, white plants. Under the moonlight the woods were a ghostly white; in the thin winter sunshine they sparkled and glittered. The land turned hard as iron.

The wildlife had a difficult time of it in this weather. Small birds – wrens, tits, goldcrests – died by the handful. The deer Taylor had seen standing in his garden at Christmas began to strip bark off the smaller trees. Mice huddled together and froze into lumps. Kites in general were not so badly affected by the cold weather. In their native Wales, a hard winter meant more dead sheep; food was plentiful.

As for Teresa, she had the gibbet. There was enough food there to get her through the longest winter, but there were other dangers. The vixen found trails hard to follow in this powdery white world, and of course could not dig in the iron ground after prey. She returned more and more often to the gibbet to feed.

And it so happened that one cold dawn in early February, she walked out of the bushes to find Teresa hanging from a frosted magpie.

Now, if a fox could laugh, that vixen laughed now. She walked openly out into the clearing and yapped, to tell the kite she was there. Teresa turned her head to watch her enemy, who stood grinning five yards away. With a whisk of her bushy red tail, the vixen walked forward and came to sit under the hanging kite. There she waited a while, to enjoy the situation better.

The fox was five or six feet beneath her. The nearest cover was four or five yards away. All Teresa could do was watch helplessly. She was entirely at the vixen's mercy. And the vixen had no mercy.

The vixen stopped grinning and shuffled on her haunches. Teresa pulled herself higher up onto the magpie she was feeding on, twisting right round to watch. The vixen stared hard, grew tense, gathered herself ... and launched herself up into the air. Her teeth snapped shut just as Teresa swayed to one side.

The fox landed and licked her lips. That first leap had decided both her and Teresa that she was more than capable of jumping that high.

The kite was hers.

As the vixen gathered herself for the next jump, Teresa in desperation twisted herself sideways, spread her wings, and launched herself into the air. It was her only chance. But once again the wing slipped out of control beneath her. She slid down in a short circle and crashed on the frostbitten ground. The fox's jaws clashed. There was a loud SNAP! as her teeth met. She twisted herself in mid-air, hit the ground, and bounced back right at the grounded bird.

But Teresa had weapons of her own. The fox ran straight into that razor sharp beak just above her eye.

The vixen yelped and drew back, a deep gash an inch long on her brow. The blood welled and flowed.

Teresa flapped and jumped again at the gibbet before the fox recovered. She made it! But now she was back where she started, six feet above the vixen, hanging off a jay this time, looking over her shoulder, waiting for the killing leap.

Licking her lips, the vixen came back under her, ready for another jump. Teresa had put up a good fight; she would do more if she could. But both of them knew how this game would end.

Then, from the trees and bushes halfway up the valley, came a loud, tuneless whistle.

Both animals looked up; it was the common enemy. A branch snapped as the man trod heavily only some twenty or thirty yards away.

Quick as a wave of the hand the fox slipped past the wall of the shed and vanished into the woods. Teresa launched herself into the air again, circled, and crashed into the long grass in the clearing. She ran like a rabbit under cover as the man came into sight.

It was not unusual for Harris to come to the gibbet this early in the morning. He was off on a business trip to Bristol, and always called by on his way past if he had the time. He did not see the vixen as she slid off, but he caught a glimpse of the great red bird as she glided round the corner of the shed. And he knew exactly what she was.

Teresa trembled in the cover of low-growing laurel as he walked right up to her. But although he had seen the first part of her brief flight, Harris had missed the crash into the grass. He thought Teresa was half a mile away by now. He had no idea that if he had stuck the muzzle of his shotgun into the bushes, he could have blasted her to mincemeat.

On the way along the gravel drive, Harris drove past Tom Mase about his rounds. The keeper had that brat of a son with him. He pulled the car over.

'Never guess what I've just seen, Mase,' he announced. 'Bloody kite, the bastard that got me hauled up and in all the papers. Tucking in at the gibbet, would you believe. Cheeky, I said!'

Tom winced and glanced at Taylor.

'The thing is, sir,' he said quickly, before Harris could go. 'After the publicity and everything ...' He shrugged. 'You understand, sir, if there's a red kite about, people will have seen it. I'd prefer not to get into trouble. Killing protected birds ... well. We've both seen where that can lead, Mr Harris.'

Harris smiled. 'See to it, won't you, Mase,' he said, as if Tom had said nothing at all. He smiled and waited for Tom's reply.

Tom met his gaze for a moment, then dropped his eyes. 'Will do, sir,' he said.

'Good lad,' said Harris. He nodded approvingly. Then he wound up the window and drove off.

Tom was red with shame. He looked down. Taylor was looking at him in disgust. He jerked his head back down the drive. 'You get back and get ready for school,' he said harshly.

'What are you going to do?' demanded Taylor.

'I'm going to do my job, if that's all right by you.'

Taylor didn't say a thing.

'Go on, scram. Get on with it!'

Taylor turned and ran home, while Tom went on to the gibbet. He was certain it must be the bird Harris had shot. Since it had been feeding here for so long there was every sign that it was wounded in some way. Chances were it couldn't go far.

He spent over an hour creeping through the trees and peering up, trying to work out where the bird was hiding. But Teresa was back in her rhododendron, tight against the trunk among the thick leaves. Tom saw nothing. He went on with his rounds; he had other work to do. He'd have another go later that morning.

For the thousandth time he damned his luck, working for Harris. He'd put out word, but not a sign of another job had he heard of. If it was him or the kite, the kite was dead meat.

At half past eight there was a thundering noise on Alan's door. Mrs James went running down the hallway again.

'SHE'S ALIVE!' howled Taylor as the door opened. Alan appeared at the end of the hallway. 'SHE'S ALIVE! SHE'S ALIVE!' screamed Alan.

'SHE'S ALIVE!' howled Taylor again. 'HARRIS HAS SEEN HER AND MY DAD'S GOING TO KILL HER...'

'WOW, TAYLOR! WOW!'

'What on earth is going on?' asked Mrs James quietly.

'WOW!'

First thing, before they went to school, the boys scrawled another letter to Teddy Harris. In the meantime they had to tell Alan's mother everything. She was amazed and scandalised when she heard the story. So the buzzard had been a kite. So they had let it go again into the wild? Wonderful! And now Tom was hunting the bird down under Harris's order?

'He could be prosecuted for doing that!' she exclaimed.

'I hope he is!' declared Taylor.

Sylvia James frowned and chewed the edge of her finger nervously. Helping the kites was one thing. But what about poor Tom? She knew him fairly well and liked him; she knew only too well how long he'd been trying to get another place. She hated to interfere with someone's job. And Taylor spoke so poisonously against his own dad! She lent the boys an envelope and a stamp for their letter, but really she was already wishing, she didn't know anything about it.

Then suddenly it was five to nine and Taylor and Alan were late for school. As his mother hurried them out of the door, Alan thrust the letter into her hand and made her promise to post it for them. He had no reason to doubt her, she was always going on about how horrible Harris was and how brutally he managed his woodland. She called goodbye from the doorstep and stared at the letter anxiously before she went back into the house.

Helping a son against his father! Putting Tom's job at risk! She should have known better. Perhaps she should tell Tom … ? But then that would be betraying Taylor. And what about the kite ... only two dozen left! It was difficult to know what to do for the best.

Later, when she was out shopping, Sylvia still hadn't made up her mind despite her promise to the boys. In the end she paused outside the post box, felt the letter with her fingers, and dropped it into the box. She felt as guilty as hell as soon as she'd done it. Poor Tom! She should have discussed it with her husband – and with Alan – before she posted it. But it was done now; the post box was like a prison with the letter inside it.

Sylvia finished her shopping and went to visit a friend. She felt awful. She wondered if she ought to give Anne Mase a ring ... but if only she'd thought of doing that before she posted the letter!

All morning Alan and Taylor sat in their classrooms and stared outside at a raw, grey world, worrying about the kite. Even now the gun could be raised, pointing, the finger tightening on the trigger.

The sky, which had been a frosty blue for days had turned overnight to a thick, even blanket of grey, full of snow. By break it had begun – big, flat, wide flakes, swaying down in the milky sky. Outside on the tarmac the other boys ran and howled and threw snowballs and made slides. Taylor and Alan stood in a corner and plotted.

'Will your dad really do as he's told?' begged Alan. He thought Tom was a wonderman. Taylor had told him so often enough, and Taylor was always right. He couldn't believe he'd do something so awful.

'He'll do it all right,' said Taylor.

Alan stared out at the swirling snowflakes, stricken with grief.

'We'd better go and find her,' he said.

'What, now?'

'But he might be killing her! You just said so.'

Taylor licked his lips nervously.

'What about school?'

'What about it?' said Alan boldly.

It was true. There were things more important than school. Saving one of the two dozen or so kites left in Britain was one of them. But Taylor hesitated and the bell rang. The boys crept back in, looking backwards into the trees. By now, the woods were just shadows against the heavily falling snow.

By half past eleven, the snow was already an inch deep and still falling. On his way home for lunch, Tom stopped by at the clearing to try again for the kite. He approached softly, but all he saw was a crow pecking at the eyes of a squirrel hanging on the shed wall. He could have had a good clear shot at it but he didn't want to frighten his real prey, if she was still about.

He checked the snow for tracks. A fall of snow like this laid the movements of the creatures of the woods and fields bare. Not a mouse, not a stoat, certainly not a great hawk trailing across the ground, could avoid leaving their marks for all to see. In the snow, Tom could almost count the animals he shared the woods with.

143

But there were no tracks. Teresa had not fed since the snow fell.

Tom made his way to look at the dead animals hanging up, then carefully walked all around the edges of the clearing, looking up in the trees, checking the snow for signs of the big bird.

In the depths of the rhododendron tree, Teresa listened to the man walking under her tree, saw him stop and peer up. Not a feather did she move. The snow lay like a blanket on the leaves and branches. Inside it was dark and safe. Tom saw nothing in the half-light, cluttered by falling snowflakes, and he passed harmlessly on.

Tom sighed and kicked the snow off his boots irritably. The whole thing was filthy. It was just a matter of time, but the sooner it was done the happier he'd be. And then there was Taylor at the other end of the day! Tom winced. He liked his son to be proud of him. He remembered the look on his face when he'd told him to run off that morning.

Well, this was the real world. If it had to be done, it had to be done. That afternoon he had to visit one of the farms Harris rented out on the edge of the woodland to discuss the use of a field Harris wanted planted with trees. Tomorrow he'd be back, though.

Another day or so and he'd have her dead and buried.

By lunch time Taylor had made up his mind. He knew how good at his job his dad was. If Teresa was there he'd find her, unless they found her first.

He found Alan queuing for his dinner in the hall.

144

'Come on. Let's go.'

'What about dinner?'

'Teresa might end up dead because of you eating your dinner!'

Alan looked at the steaming puddles of brown slop and the chalky, lumpy tablets of mashed potato.

'Yeah … let's go,' he agreed.

They left the hall one at a time as if they were going to the toilet. They met in the cloakroom and ran across the playground through the trodden snow onto School Lane. They ran like rabbits until they were out of sight of the village and then hurried on along the road to the woods, sliding on the new snow and hiding whenever a car went by.

The snow in the clearing was smooth and unbroken but for one set of prints. Taylor walked in his father's footsteps to the gibbet. He didn't think about what Tom was doing, or how he let himself be humiliated by Harris. He told himself that it was Harris who was to blame, that it was Harris he hated, not his dad. But he felt betrayed all the same.

Alan found a deep snowdrift against one side of the shed and spent the first few minutes jumping in and out of it.

'You'll make yourself wet and then you'll have to go home,' said Taylor scornfully as Alan disappeared up to his waist.

'Won't,' said Alan. But he was suddenly aware that his boots were full of snow, and he quickly nipped round the corner to empty them before Taylor spotted him.

'Here ... here ... here!' said Taylor excitedly. He was looking at the wall where the dead creatures hung. 'Al ... see what I've found.'

Alan came bounding round with one welly off and fell over.

'She's been feeding. See?'

Alan put his boot on – his foot felt horrid – and together they stared at the shredded remains of the jays on the gibbet.

'She's here,' said Taylor. 'I told you. Definitely!'

Both boys turned around and looked behind at the snowy trees. Was she there, hidden, watching them? The snowflakes fell, twisting and floating on the air. There was no other movement.

Taylor called, 'Teresa? Teresa?' Even his voice seemed to turn to snow in the air around him. Alan had a go. 'Here ... PUSS, PUSS, PUSS!' he bellowed, far too loud. A couple of pigeons leapt out of a nearby tree and clattered off.

'Shut up, you'll scare her!' hissed Taylor.

'You shouted,' said Alan indignantly.

'I didn't yell like Tarzan of the Apes,' scolded Taylor. He rolled his eyes. Alan was like a badly trained puppy. 'Come on, let's search. I'll do those trees over there and you do that side.'

They marched across the deep snow to the edges of the clearing. For over an hour they wandered about the borders of the clearing, peering up, calling softly, climbing up onto the lower branches for a better look. They went deeper into the woods but they saw nothing but the snow steadily falling, falling, falling. Everything else was still.

They came back to the gibbet. By now Alan was moaning with cold and hunger. 'Is it time to go home, Taylor? I'm so hungry, Taylor. I could eat one of those jays!'

'Ugh, you perv,' groaned Taylor. Actually, he was starving himself. Maybe they should have waited and eaten their dinners after all.

'Do you reckon school's over yet?' asked Alan nervously. He wasn't looking forward to going home in case he'd been found out. But he wanted to go and get a sandwich or something. His feet were frozen like lumps of ice.

'Not while it's still light. It's almost dark by the time we get out of school, remember?' said Taylor. He didn't say anything to Alan, but he was pretty certain that Tom would come back sooner or later to have another go for Teresa. Even if he didn't find them there, there were the prints from their wellies all around the clearing and in the surrounding woods. But he wasn't going to let that stop him. Let Tom find out. It was Taylor who was doing the right thing, and his dad knew it.

They decided to sit hidden among the trees and wait for her to come out. That way, even if Tom came he wouldn't catch them at once. They found a place to settle down under the eaves of a hawthorn bush with dirty red berries hanging on it.

It was hard sitting in the hawthorn bush. It was so cold and lonely among the trees and the snow once you stopped talking. It all seemed so sad. It got colder and colder and colder. Alan's feet were so numb he felt that he had to balance on them as if they were lumps of something else when he stood up.

'Hey, guess what? I can't feel my toes.'

'Shut up about your toes.'

Another five minutes went by.

'Do you think I've got frostbite?'

'Shut up.'

'I bet when I walk we'll hear my toes rattling about in my boots.'

'You'll hear your teeth rattling around my knuckles if you don't shut up.'

Another five minutes. The snow fell off. Just a few flakes fell now, softly stirring in the sky. It was beginning to get dark. The boys huddled up into their coats and listened for Teresa, and stared at the snow until their eyes hurt.

'What about if we get down a jay or something and walk around calling to her?' suggested Alan at last.

They trudged back to the shed and took down a jay. Alan was getting sulky. He followed Taylor round as he walked the edges of the woods holding the stiff, still body aloft and nagged at him.

'Teresa! Teresa! … Dinner! Here, puss, puss, puss! Here, puss!' Taylor called. His words were swallowed up by the snow.

'Come on, let's go.'

'Here, puss!'

'She's not here.'

'Shut up. Puss! Puss!' Taylor walked up to the trees with his dead jay.

'But she's not here!'

And… she called …

'Hi-hi-ya …' Just once. The sound floated out of the dark trees like a spell cast over the snowy night, and then was gone. So quick – a single second and everything was as it had been before. But it was different. Teresa was there.

'Was it her?'

'You know it was!' They were speaking in whispers in case they scared her.

'Where did it come from?'

'I don't know, I don't know!'

'I'll try again…'

Taylor lifted up the jay. 'Here, puss, puss, puss!'

Silence.

'It *was* her, wasn't it?'

'… I think it came from over there.'

Alan pointed to the rhododendron. Taylor walked softly towards it, calling.

'Teresa … please, Teresa, are you there?'

'Puss, puss, puss!' called Alan.

There was a slight noise in the tree ahead of them. The boys walked, oh so softly, underneath it and peered up. Taylor stood still on the ground holding his jay in the air, while Alan carefully climbed the first few branches.

'I see her!'

'Where?'

'There! There! See?'

Taylor came to stand on the thick branch next to his friend and peered up into the dusty, snowy bones of the tree. From up high a pair of great yellow eyes looked down. The sharp beak opened.

'Hi-hi-heea!'

'Teresa! Yes! Yes!'

'You darling!'

Taylor and Alan danced a high stepping dance and flung handfuls of snow in the air. It was a miracle. After everything! She was still alive!

It was one thing seeing her. Catching her was another matter.

They tried luring her down with the jay. She called greedily, but wouldn't come. When they tried to climb up to her she got nervous and began climbing away from them, fluttering and stamping on the branches. When she opened her wings to balance they could see how crooked the left one was.

'I don't think she can fly ...'

Alan, who could go faster in the small branches high up, reached up higher. He was within a few feet, but just as he got close, she fluttered and jumped, fluttered and jumped ... and there, she'd crossed over into another tree, across the barrier of small twigs where he couldn't follow.

It was so frustrating, and it was getting darker by the minute. They tried leaving the jay on the ground near her tree and going out of sight. She cried to them desperately as they disappeared but she was too scared to come down.

'You stupid bloody bird!' yelled Taylor. She didn't want them to go, she didn't want to come. What did she want?

The two boys started to quarrel about what to do next, whether to go home and come back tomorrow, or to try again. It was dark and still and they would have heard the feet crunch over the snow normally. But they were so engrossed that they didn't notice anything until a beam of light swung across the clearing and picked them out.

'What the bloody hell are you doing here!' It was Harris.

'Mr Harris! I'm … on a job for my father …'

Harris stamped up through the snow. He had a powerful torch in one hand and a large black shopping bag in the other. He swung the beam from face to face, standing in front of them like a lump of darkness.

'And what about you?' he demanded, shining the light in Alan's eyes. 'On a job for his father too, are you?'

'Er…'

'You're a bloody little trespasser!' Harris reached out and pinched Alan's ear hard. The ear was cold; it hurt. 'Get out of here. And you. There'll be no more jobs for anyone if you use that as an excuse to trespass on my property. Go on … scram!'

The two boys hurried off through the snow. Harris snorted with disgust. He held them in his beam until they were out of sight.

When all sound of them had died away, Harris stamped his way over to the gibbet. He put the shopping bag on the ground and took out a little bottle of white powder and a kitchen knife.

151

Taking the knife, he grabbed hold of one of the jays hanging upside down on the gibbet and stabbed it between the legs. He pushed the knife in, making a deep wound. Then, very carefully he tapped a few grains of the white powder into the wound. He pushed the edges of the cut closed. Then he moved on to the next bird … and the next.

When he was done he put his things back in the bag and washed his hands anxiously in the snow until they were chapped. He was scared in case the poison had touched his skin. Then he rubbed his icy hands together and hissed irritably. He didn't trust Mase to do the job, so he was making sure for himself that the kite got killed. But what was the point of having a gamekeeper who didn't keep game? Why pay wages to work yourself?

'Bloody, holier-than-thou, bloody Mase,' he growled. He'd start keeping an eye open for a better man after this, that was for sure.

Harris turned and made his way back through the woods to his car.

The next day was a Saturday. First light found Taylor peering through his curtains. He had to use his nails to scratch away the frosty patterns on the glass. The sky was clear and the land was so white it hurt your eyes. Just a few tiny flakes whipped past his window on a frozen wind. Everything had been sculpted by the wind into drifts and gullies, as if the garden and the woods had flown in from another planet.

Today Teddy Harris would get the letter. He might be here by this evening, if he could make his way through the snow.

Taylor shivered violently and did a dance. His room was freezing! He grabbed his clothes and ran downstairs to dress by the Aga where it was always warm.

Five minutes later his mum came down to find him pulling on his boots.

'And where are you off to?'

'Alan'll be here in a minute.'

'Breakfast first, my pet.'

'I'll have some toast.'

'You'll have bacon and egg with the rest of us. A morning like this, you need a bit of fuel to burn up.'

'But what about Alan?'

'Alan can wait. Or he can have a spot to eat with us.'

Taylor bit his lip. What could he say? A moment later his father came down, yawning in his dressing-gown. Taylor watched him anxiously. Had he found the giveaway marks of his and Alan's boots in the snow?

'No work for you today, my lad,' said Anne Mase, giving her husband a squeeze and a kiss.

'Maybe,' said Tom. Over his wife's shoulder, he caught Taylor's eye and held it. But he said nothing.

'You can spend a little time with me, Mister. There's nothing you can do in this lot.'

Tom smiled and put his arm round her waist. Taylor's heart jumped. He'd have the whole day to catch Teresa. 'Except I'll have to take the dogs out, of course,' added

Tom. And once again he caught Taylor's eye. He raised his eyebrows slightly, as if to say – not so lucky after all.

Half an hour later, while Taylor was gobbling down his eggs and bacon, Teddy Harris was sitting in his kitchen in Taunton slicing the top off his boiled egg and sorting through his mail. Here was one from Hale Magna! Mmm … the Mase boy! How nice …

Teddy had his own housekeeper. Mrs Brennan was used by now to all the strange noises Teddy made as he went about his business. Where most people whistled tunes they'd heard on the radio, Teddy warbled bird song. It had been a bit of a shock for her at first. She'd been mopping the kitchen floor when she heard a gorgeous songbird pouring out its heart in an upstairs room.

Poor, sweet thing, it must've flown in through a window, thought Mrs Brennan, and she ran upstairs to sort if out. She tracked the bird by ear down the hall, flung open the door … to find Mr Harris perched on the toilet with his shorts round his ankles and his lips pursed. He clutched the bowl and yelped in surprise. Mrs Brennan slammed the door shut with a bang.

'Sorry, Mr Harris. I think there's a nightingale trapped in the toilet!'

'That's not a nightingale, that's me!' exclaimed the old man.

Mrs Brennan had heard everything: owls hooting in the sitting room, ravens croaking on the landing, buzzards mewing in the bathroom, as well as nightingales in the

154

toilet. Even so she was surprised to hear a great howling in the kitchen at eight o'clock in the morning.

'Oh, Lord, I've never heard that one before,' she exclaimed, clutching at the sink in surprise.

'That was me! There's a kite! There's a kite!' howled Teddy. And he went bounding into the hall to the telephone.

He had to get to Hale, but the snow lay three inches deep on his window-sill. The journey could take hours! He was lucky that the letter had got through at all. First he must ring up Harris and let him know that he was on his way.

And if only Teddy had opened his mail before breakfast, he might have been in time to stop Harris.

'Oh, I'm sorry, Mr Harris, but he's already up and about. He said he was off to inspect the gibbet. There's been trespassers, apparently. He left about, oh … fifteen minutes ago.'

'If anything happens to that bird I'll hold him personally responsible,' snarled Teddy. 'You tell him, Mrs Dell. He knows! I'll cut him off without a penny!'

'I'll make sure he gets the message, sir, as soon as he gets back.'

'And, Mrs Dell … do you think you could get a message down to Taylor and his dad? Let them know, I'm on my way!'

Teddy slammed down the phone and rushed up to pack his bag. Soon, clutching a packed lunch and a Thermos made up by Mrs Brennan, he rushed out to his car and started wiping three inches of snow off the windscreen and bonnet. He jumped in, turned the key, and the poor old thing wheezed softly to itself.

It was another hour by the time Teddy pulled out of the drive and pushed his way through the snow and up the road. The drive would take hours. The roads might well be impassable.

But it didn't make any difference after all. It was already too late.

Fifteen

Hours before, Teresa was already easing her shoulders out of the leaves at the edge of the rhododendron bush and looking hungrily down at the poisoned bait Harris had left out for her.

Yesterday, what with the snow, with Tom in the morning and Taylor and Alan in the afternoon, she hadn't had a chance to get down to the gibbet to feed. It had been a hard night and the harsh wind soaked up what warmth there was in a second. Like Taylor, the birds needed extra food to keep warm in this kind of weather.

Teresa was starving hungry.

She peered past the thick, rubbery leaves, piled high with snow, down across the white air to the gibbet. The shed wall was covered with bushy white moustaches where the snow had settled on the ledges of a hundred little corpses.

It was dark, hooded with snow, inside her hideaway tree. Teresa leaned forward, opening her mouth and blinking at the white light. She was plucking up her courage to take the daily risk with her life, down to the ground to snatch her food.

A slight noise made her pause and look across the trees. Red flickered briefly. A moment later, a little further along, the face of the vixen pushed out of cover. She looked this way, that way, before jumping into the clearing, and she sank at once up to her chest in snow.

The vixen was hungry, too. It was hard work hunting for mice and rabbits in this. The gibbet was far easier. The meat there didn't try to get away.

She made her way across the clearing in a series of high leaps to clear the snow. The icy wind had frozen a crust of ice on the surface, and she cracked and crunched her way painfully forward. Once she got into the shelter of the old shed wall, the snow was thin and it was easier. Shaking herself, she looked around again to check that all was well. She caught sight of Teresa staring down at her from her hiding place, but took no notice. The need for food was too great to play games today.

She made a quick jump and grabbed a fat crow. It took her a couple of goes to drag it off its nail. Straight away she bounded back along her own tracks. The crow was frozen stiff and its wings stuck out, so that when she was up to her shoulders in the snow, her nose looked like some sort of strange red bird with black wings flying in the snow.

The vixen disappeared swiftly into the woods. She would eat her crow hidden away, and then lie up for the rest of the day.

Teresa waited until the fox was out of sight, then waited again. Down in the clearing a pair of crows appeared, circling silently just above the trees. One landed heavily under the gibbet; the other landed directly on top of a jay, and began pecking, short hard blows to the skull of the frozen bird.

In weather like this, with everything under snow and frozen like iron, the gibbet was the only source of food for miles around for many birds and beasts. Harris had chosen the exact worst time to put out his poison. As Teresa watched a magpie come to join the feast, the vixen was chewing her crow soft under the floor of a shed a quarter of a mile away. The eating of this would put an end to all her fine ways. Within five minutes she felt the first cramps. Within ten she was retching. and whining from the violent pains in her stomach. In half an hour she was dead, stiffening slowly under the rotting floorboards as ice formed on the vomit from her last meal. No longer quick and bright and red and clever, she was simply disgusting.

This was to be a last supper for many of the birds and beasts in the woods that day. Vixen, crows, magpie, the rats who lived in the gibbet shed – they were all doomed. One peck was enough. The poison was deadly. A man handling the victims after would be advised to wear gloves and still to wash his hands after merely touching them.

Teresa hungrily watched the crows and the magpie pecking at the soft parts of the creatures hanging on the wall. Ravenous though she was she did not yet jump down to join the feast. The other birds would mob her if they found her in the open, and she was not able to fly away.

At long, last the crows flew off, the magpie cackled in alarm at some noise in the bushes and took to the air. Teresa checked again – scent, sight and sound. Look, listen, smell. This was a lot more dangerous than crossing the road. Only when she was really sure that everything was still did she push herself out into an opening in the leaves. She peered around yet again, her sharp eyes searching for signs of movement. Then at last she jumped out of the tree, held her wings out and parachuted down to the ground.

It was a while now since Teresa's wing had healed but she still hadn't got used to what happened when she tried to fly. It took her by surprise every time. The air beneath her played a trick. Instead of gliding smoothly down towards the shed, she went in a wide circle. The ground rushed forward, and Teresa crashed head first into a deep drift of snow that had gathered along a felled tree in the middle of the clearing. She hit it with some force, cracked the crust of ice on the surface and disappeared completely under the snow.

For a second Teresa was shocked into stillness. What had happened to the ground? Why was it suddenly up around her shoulders? Then she panicked. She scrabbled with her feet on the soft snow. But the ice crust held her down and the soft stuff underneath gave way under her feet. Gradually, though, she trampled the snow firmly under her and made a hole big enough for her to get her head and neck and part of her shoulders out above the snow.

She peered this way and that, her mouth open. She was terrified that she would be caught like this. The fox, a cat, a man – anything could take her now. There was no thought of food now. She had to get out before someone came.

Teresa tried to open her wings and after some effort, got them above the snow. Using her wings and her feet, she half ploughed, half pushed her way through the top layer of snow, cracking the ice crust with her chest. She was out of the worst of the drift now but the snow was still nearly nine inches deep. There was no option but to plough on through it if she wanted to get away. The work was exhausting. There were five yards or more to go before she reached the cover of the trees where the snow would be thin enough for her to walk properly. She could be discovered at any minute.

She fought, struggled, paused to rest, fought again. Her whole chest now was stinging with the cold ... but she was getting there. The ice was breaking, the snow was melting and wetting her feathers, but inch by inch she was getting closer to the cover of the trees, and the safety of her tree.

It was at this moment that she heard the human voices.

Teresa lay dark on the white surface like a target. The people were coming through the trees. But she knew them! Humans were enemies – but not all humans. Once these people had been friends ...

In a panic of recognition and hope she screamed out to Taylor and Alan as she had when she was a chick. Help! Help me! Hi-hi-hiiiea!

The two boys had bolted their breakfasts and got togged up to go out in double-quick time.

'Let's go sledging!' exclaimed Alan suddenly at the back

door, in ecstasy at the sight of all that perfect, untouched snow.

Taylor just looked at him as if he was made out of dung.

'Sorry, Taylor,' said Alan.

Taylor stamped off up the drive with Alan trailing after him sulkily. Taylor was no fun sometimes. But they did pause on the way for a snowball fight, and to shake the snow off the overhanging branches edging the woodland down onto each other's heads.

As they got near the clearing the two boys planned how to catch Teresa. Taylor thought one of them should climb her tree while the other climbed the tree next to her. Then one could chase her into the other's arms. But Alan was scared about meeting Harris again. He was trying to convince Taylor they ought to leave it to Teddy Harris, who could be there at any time. He only lived in Taunton, not that far away at all.

They were still chattering away when they came to the smaller trees at the edge of the clearing. Then, two things happened.

The first thing was Teresa calling. The sound cut through their chatter like a knife. They understood at once that this was a cry for help, a desperate cry. They ran suddenly forward and burst out from under the low trees at the clearing's edge into the snow. They stood for a second, taking in the scene, looking for signs of Teresa. Opposite them, on the other side of the clearing, the bushes shook, the snow fell … and Harris stepped into view.

Alan squeaked in shock. Everything froze.

Harris stood there with his gun over his forearm, his jaw jutting slightly out. He had heard the boys ... and the bird. He'd been waiting in hiding for them to show themselves.

'I'll bloody sack your father if he can't keep control of you, you disobedient little sod,' he said quietly.

Taylor glanced sideways. Where was she? But Harris terrified him.

'As for you ...' Harris swung his gun lazily towards Alan. 'James, isn't it? You can get back home and wait for the police. I warned you once. Trespass! I don't want to see either of you in these woods again. Understand?'

'Sir!' Alan backed off, but Taylor still lingered, gulping, caught between fear and desire. He saw Harris glance sideways at something to one side, hidden by a corner of the shed. He took two steps forward – and there she was! There she was!

'Get!' screamed Harris. Alan fled, but Taylor still hung on. She was so still! Was it already too late? He took another step forward, just in time to see her head lift. She called out again. Hi-hi-hiea! Help! Don't leave me! Don't go!

'Get out of here!' bawled Harris, in a real rage, and he bounded violently forward at the boy. Taylor stumbled, turned, and fled after his friend. Suddenly he was haring through the woods. It was too late, it was too late. But he had seen her alive! How could he leave her to Harris?

Taylor skidded to a halt, determined to go back despite his fear. But then behind him he heard the terrifying roar of the gun going off. He heard Alan crashing through the trees ahead of him. He called out, 'Al!' and he was running after him, skidding and crashing and bumping through the woods, as if the devil had his claw on him.

Harris had spotted the kite as soon as he entered the clearing. She lay still and dark against the snow. He could see her out of the corner of his eye as he bawled out the two boys. He was furious with Taylor for seeing her as well as for not obeying at once. By the time the boy ran off, Harris was panting with anger.

Having to play hide-and-seek with his gamekeeper's son! The gamekeeper himself questioning his orders. And to cap it all, last night he had had a phone call from Alan's father, who had made it clear that he knew there was a kite in the woods, and that Harris was responsible for its welfare.

So now he was supposed to be a nursemaid for vermin!

It didn't take much imagination to work out where Mr and Mrs James had got their information from either. Taylor and his little friend had a lot to answer for.

And now he was on his own with the bird.

Harris lifted his gun in the air and fired off one barrel. The kite was already dead, as far as everyone else was concerned. For his part, he wanted to have a good look at it before he gave it the other barrel. But use the other barrel he most certainly would.

He reloaded, standing in the snow and glancing at the kite. He'd thought at first she was dead with the poison, but at the sound of the gun she began to struggle desperately in her little prison of snow. She glanced after

Taylor. Her mouth opened. She looked up at the man towering over her like a giant.

'Ho, ho, ho,' said Harris. He watched as her struggles quickly died; she was exhausted. He walked across to the stranded bird. She struggled again, briefly.

Harris stood above her. He could have crushed her with his foot. He could have blasted her to shreds there and then. But Harris was a shooting man. He wanted a decent shot.

'GET UP!' he yelled suddenly at the top of his big voice. He wanted her to fly so he could blast her down. The kite struggled and beat her wings, but she couldn't fly, not even to escape Harris.

Harris might have thrown her into the air to get her going if he hadn't been scared she might peck his hands. Instead, he lifted his boot and gave her a great kick, digging his foot down right underneath her. Teresa tumbled out of the snow like a clod of earth and fell on her back. Harris raised his gun. Painfully the kite struggled to her feet and turned to face him. She raised her wings, fluffed out her feathers, opened her mouth, did everything she could to make herself huge and fearsome.

'Dear, oh dear,' said Harris. He took a couple of steps sideways and then ran at her and gave her another huge kick. He watched the great bird soar gracelessly through the air and roll over in the snow. She was helpless. He walked over and gave her another, and another, and another, and another, until at last she lay in the snow not moving at all.

Panting with the effort, Harris came to inspect his work. The kite was broken.

'Not many birdwatchers around today,' said Harris.

He wasn't sure if the bird was dead or not, so he wrapped his handkerchief around his hand before he bent down and picked her up by her feet. She hung there, her head dangling from her limp neck. A drip of blood fell out of her beak and lay bright red on the snow.

'We'll see you fly.'

He carried her over to the gibbet and found the hammer and nails Tom used to nail up the vermin. He couldn't see the string, so instead he drove the nail through the thick bone above her foot. As he did it, the pain awoke Teresa, who weakly flapped her wings and screamed once.

Harris turned and took twenty steps back and turned to face her.

The kite hung crucified by her foot, upside down, her wings open.

'Spot of target practice,' said Harris. He raised the shotgun and took aim.

Tom and Anne Mase had a long slow breakfast, then did the dishes together, listening to pop hits on the radio.

After that, Anne wanted to go back to bed; it wasn't often they had long drifts of time to themselves.

But work or play, Tom had his dogs. They needed breakfast, too, and a bit of a run after being cooped up all night. He and Anne could hear them scratching at the door of the kennel shed beside the house and barking. Come on! Come on! Hurry up!

'I'll be half an hour,' he promised. 'Put the fire on up there.' He shrugged, she pulled a face, but they both knew the dogs had to be done.

Tom put on his coat, let the dogs out, and set out down the snowy drive into the woods. The first thing he saw in the snow outside was Taylor and Alan's footprints. He knew exactly where they were heading.

Tom sighed unhappily. It was a miserable business. Just his luck that Taylor should have been with him when Harris told him about the kite!

He followed the tracks along the drive and off into the woods for a while. He ought to deal with this. But it was a messy business, one he had no appetite for. And there was Anne waiting at home for him.

Tom stopped and stood in the snow, breathing in the cold, white air. The dogs shuffled in the snow and looked impatiently at him.

There was nothing anyone could do anyway.

As he stood there undecided, Tom heard shouting in the woods ahead. A man: Harris. Then Taylor. Harris had caught them poking about! There'd be hell to pay!

Tom waited grimly, listening to the sounds of the boys running towards him. There was a gunshot. What on earth was Harris playing at? He ordered the dogs to sit and wait and began to walk towards the sounds ahead of him.

The first Taylor knew of his dad being there was Alan. He heard him cry out, 'Mr Mase! Mr Mase! Stop him! Stop him!'

167

For a second his heart leapt with hope. His dad could do something if anyone could! He put on a burst of speed and pushed his way forward, past the icy twigs whipping at his face. He crashed through some bushes. Alan was bending, panting with the run, his hands on his knees. 'Harris has got the kite. Harris …'

Then he saw his father's still face and he remembered. It was a waste of time.

Tom nodded back the other way. 'You run home,' he said curtly. 'I'll … have a look.' Even as he spoke he was aware how weak it sounded.

'You can't do anything,' said Taylor.

'Get back home,' said his dad sharply.

Taylor watched him as he pushed his way in between the trees. 'It's too late, anyhow,' he shouted. 'It's too late!' There were tears on his face as he turned to lead Alan back home.

Tom was smarting badly. He was ashamed at the way Harris treated him and the way he obeyed. The scorn in his son's voice was still stinging him as he arrived at the edge of the clearing. He was just in time to see Harris carry the bird to the gibbet.

Seeing Harris with the bird, Tom at once took a step back, hiding himself among the trees. He was thinking, thank God it wasn't him who was doing it. It would be easier for Tom if he could tell Taylor, yes, it had been too late. But Tom glanced over his shoulder as he did it. How awful if his son were to see him hiding!

Tom was hoping that the bird was dead, but when Harris drove the nail into the kite's foot she screamed like a girl. Tom was horrified. The hair prickled on the back of his head, and he blushed red with shame. He remembered how his father had once caught him kicking frogs over the hedge, and whipped him for it.

Hardly thinking, Tom began to walk forward. He had no idea what his boss was up to until he saw him turn and raise the gun. Then without thinking about it he put up his hand and bawled, 'Mr Harris!'

Harris almost leapt out of his trousers. He turned to watch the man walking through the snow towards him without putting the gun down. For a moment he was speechless. Even Harris felt humiliated to be caught behaving like this.

He gulped and got his words back. 'I'm my own bloody gamekeeper now, Mase,' he told him. 'Look at Pretty Polly now.' He grinned and suddenly his shame was replaced by rage. Who did the man think he was?

He turned back to his gun. Tom took three more steps, reached out and pushed the barrel down into the snow.

'What the bloody hell do you think you're playing at, Mase? You stand back!'

But Tom had put his back in between him and the kite. He ignored the armed man hissing with rage behind him and walked the few yards to where the kite was hanging.

'That's a bloody, stupid thing to do, Mase. I could have taken your stupid head off. Get out of my way!'

Tom reached Teresa and found the nail hammered

through her foot. He glanced in disgust at Harris, who stood there, red with embarrassment and rage.

'You're the vermin, Mr Harris,' said Tom. He took his pocket knife from his pocket and levered the nail out. The kite flapped twice, weakly. He peeled off his scarf and wrapped it round her and tucked her under his arm.

Harris's face was as white as the snow.

'The land would be cleared of your kind if I had my way,' said Tom. 'It's you'd be hung by your heels and shot.'

'You're sacked,' said Harris in disgust.

As Tom walked past him Harris began to swear and bluster, ordering him to put the bird down. It was his property, it was on his land, he could do what he wanted with it. Tom took no notice. As he got back onto the drive, he could hear explosions behind him. Harris was taking out his temper by blasting at the dead animals on the gibbet, punching hole after hole into the wooden shed wall.

Taylor was in the kitchen with Alan and his mother when Mrs Dell came round with the message from Teddy Harris. So Teddy had rung Harris to stop him – fifteen minutes too late. Everything was against Teresa, even time. All Teddy could do now was scold his nephew and there'd be another fine. None of that would bring back the lost bird.

Then the door opened and there was his father. Taylor stared in horror at the straggle of feathers hanging limply under his arm and rose out of his seat. Why had he

170

brought the carcass home? But then the carcass lifted up its head and squeaked at him in recognition.

'Thanks, Dad,' said Taylor in surprise. And he burst into tears.

Half an hour later, Mr Cantor the vet rubbed his face and got to his feet. Teresa was wrapped in a blanket in front of the Aga, pecking weakly at a lump of mutton.

'She'll live. But she'll never fly again,' said the vet.

'So we've lost our house and our income for the sake of one crippled bird.' Anne Mase glared at her husband and at her son; she didn't know which one she was crosser with.

Taylor shrugged. He had no idea how difficult all this was going to be.

'There was no choice, really,' said Tom. 'When I saw what Harris was doing ... Well. You can put up with so much ...' And he glanced shyly at Taylor, who was smiling angelically at him. Tom nodded his head and looked grim; but inside he was just delighted to have his son's adoration back.

'Wow, Taylor, your dad's a hero!' exclaimed Alan.

A little smile flickered on Tom's face.

Despite herself, Anne couldn't help smiling at Taylor and his dad smirking like that at one another. But then she sighed irritably.

'All this fuss,' she muttered.

Mr Cantor scratched his ear. 'Well ... I'd better be getting on.'

'Oh, no! You'd better stay for a cuppa, after coming out in all this. Who wants a cuppa?' She began to bang around, filling the kettle, putting it on the stove.

'After that, Taylor and Alan can come with me down to the police station,' said Tom. 'We have something to report to Constable Vanes. Right, lads?'

'Right, Dad!'

Tom looked at Teresa, who had fallen asleep in her box by the fire. 'She's a tough old thing. Whatever happens to Harris they can't take his land off him. There'll be no home for her round here.'

'Teddy Harris'll find a place for her,' said Taylor confidently. The old man was on his way; he'd get it sorted.

'Very nice for Teresa,' said his mum, rattling the mugs down on the Aga to get them warm. 'What I want to know is, who's going to find a place for us?'

'I've lived here all my life,' said Taylor suddenly. He was trying to imagine living somewhere else, but he couldn't do it.

It was such an odd thing for him to say. Tom looked curiously at him.

'Well, we were only here on sufferance after all,' he said. 'Just like her.' He nodded at Teresa, who had settled down in her place, full of mutton, warm from the fire, and half closed her eyes to go to sleep.

Afterword

Red kites used to be common in England, Scotland and Wales. In medieval times one of the famous sights of London was that of kites tearing the flesh off the bodies of felons displayed on London Bridge. Right up to the end of the eighteenth century they were still familiar, but with the practice of breeding game birds for sport came the rise of the profession of gamekeeping and the persecution began. By 1900 there were apparently only a dozen birds left, nesting in a single valley in mid-Wales.

Despite much time and money spent, they hung on over the next sixty years by the most precariously thin thread you can imagine. Numbers varied between three and ten pairs ... up and down, up and down ... never increasing enough to escape danger, never quite disappearing. Recent work on genetics has shown that all the surviving British birds are descended from a single female.

At last, in the late sixties, the kites began to recover and by the mid-seventies there were over a hundred birds. It seems likely that the last Welsh birds escaped only by being so willing to desert the nest, but this same trait made it terribly difficult for them to find new nesting sites. The problem has been helped by the introduction of new blood from the Spanish and Swedish populations and now, for the first time in over a hundred years, the red kite is in no immediate danger.

So the kites made it – but only just. To have sunk so very low for so very long … in a reasonable world they should certainly have become extinct. That they survived at all is something of a miracle. But it is a miracle brought about by people – the great many of them who worked so hard, and against such odds, for so many years, to bring this wonderful creature back from the brink of destruction.